Indonesia

Indonesia

BY TAMRA ORR

Enchantment of the World
Second Series

Children's Press®

A Division of Scholastic Inc.

NEW YORK TORONTO LONDON AUCKLAND SYDNEY
MEXICO CITY NEW DELHI HONG KONG
DANBURY, CONNECTICUT

Frontispiece: Pura Ulun Danu temple, Bali

Consultant: Dr. Gretchen Weix, Department of Anthropology, University of Montana–Missoula

Please note: All statistics are as up-to-date as possible at the time of publication.

Book production by Herman Adler Design

Library of Congress Cataloging-in-Publication Data

Orr, Tamra.
    Indonesia / by Tamra Orr. — 1st ed.
      p. cm. — (Enchantment of the world. Second series)
    Includes bibliographical references and index.
    ISBN 0-516-23684-9
    1. Indonesia—Juvenile literature. I. Title. II. Series.
DS615.O77 2005
959.8—dc22   2004015561

CHILDREN'S PRESS and associated logos are trademarks and or registered
trademarks of Scholastic Library Publishing. SCHOLASTIC and associated logos
are trademarks and or registered trademarks of Scholastic Inc.
1 2 3 4 5 6 7 8 9 10 R 14 13 12 11 10 09 08 07 06 05

Indonesia

Cover photo:
Javanese dancer

Contents

Borobudur

Wayang shadow puppet

A Sparkling Jewel

It comes as little surprise that the 18,000 islands that make up Indonesia were once compared to an emerald necklace. Those green gems that stretch out across the blue sea have attracted attention from pirates to soldiers, to mining companies and tourists. In many ways, Indonesia seems to have it all: ethnic groups that span every possible kind of culture, beautiful beaches, magnificent mountains, and volatile volcanoes.

Only 6,000 of the archipelago, or group of islands, are presently inhabited. Despite this, there is great diversity of people, flora, and fauna. Everything from tigers and leopards to sea turtles and Komodo dragons can be found in Indonesia, in addition to the world's largest—and smelliest—flower and huge walking stick insects.

Among the thousands of islands are millions of people. Together they create a modern nation of Indonesians. Even though they are spread out across the ocean, they share the same language: Bahasa Indonesia. Most of them also share the same religion, as 80 percent are Muslim. Small cultures that believe in spirits, gods, and demons are also found here, along with rural farmers and fishing communities. Other areas are full of bustling cities and multiple tourist attractions. Still others are

Opposite: **The thousands of islands that are Indonesia are home to sandy beaches, lofty mountains, turbulent volcanoes, as well as various cultures and peoples.**

This Dayak shaman performs a ceremonial dance. The Dayak tribe believes in spirits and animism.

somewhere in between, offering fascinating peeks into a truly unique country.

The main islands of Indonesia are Bali, Java, Sumatra, Kalimantan, Sulawesi, and Irian Jaya. Bali usually conjures up pictures of a beach lover's paradise, and for years it has been a top choice for vacationers who want to get away from it all. That image is not far from the truth. Bali has everything from majestic volcanoes and lush forests to soaring temples and warm, sunny beaches. It is home to most of the Hindus in Indonesia.

Java is the most developed island in Indonesia, and it features traffic jams, high-rise buildings, country scenes, and serene farms. Although most of its residents are Islamic, the Hindu-Buddhist influence can still be found here in a variety of architectural masterpieces.

Indonesia's largest city, and also its capital, is Jakarta on Java.

The island of Sumatra is the definition of tropical. It features every possible kind of scenery imaginable, from humid rain forests and muddy mangrove swamps to colorful flowers and wild creatures. Unfortunately, in the middle of all this beauty there is also the risk of earthquakes, and rumblings are not unfamiliar to its inhabitants.

Two of the islands found in Indonesia do not belong completely to that country. Only half of Timor and Papua are Indonesian. Inhabitants just step over an invisible boundary and enter a different country.

Each island of this beautiful emerald necklace holds amazing beauty, but like any place on the planet, it is the people that make it truly unique. The culture of Indonesia is far different from the United States, and those differences are fascinating.

Palm trees and lush vegetation surround a small village in Sumatra.

Women shop at a market in Sumatra. Bargaining over the price of an item is not uncommon here.

Any traveler to Indonesia soon learns that regardless of what island he is on, some of its streets are certain to be named after Indonesian heroes, kings, and kingdoms. Those streets are never completely silent. Sounds come from the shuffling footsteps of the predawn riser on his way to pray at a nearby mosque or the rapid feet of athletes trying to make a new personal best. Smelly, noisy trucks may battle to find road room around rowdy roosters as the sun rises. As the day wears on, women take over the streets as they chat, shop, sell, and gossip with others. Schoolchildren in uniforms come and go from classes; food stalls line the streets as vendors call out their offers of ethnic treats. Sidewalks are filled with pedestrians, candy wagons, street barbers, and ice storage boxes.

On every side of the street, some form of bargaining occurs. The larger stores may have fixed prices, but not smaller ones or street stalls. Indonesians often have a variety of prices on their wares; the cost depends on the customer. Bartering is encouraged, and with these islanders, it is almost an art form. Shopping is a slow, relaxed process that frequently involves as much socializing as it does business. A price is suggested and the customer may exclaim, "*Masa!*" or "Impossible." This indicates that the price is ridiculously high. When a customer suggests a different price, the seller may exclaim, "*Rugi!*" which means "Loss!" He may seem horrified to lose so much

money on a deal. However, the customer who shrugs his shoulders and begins to walk away will almost certainly be followed and the deal accepted. Once a price is reached and agreed on, it is truly bad manners for either the seller or the buyer not to follow through.

Exploring Indonesia is a delight, as island after island reveals unexpected surprises and its streets come alive with the country's unique smells, sounds, and street talk. *Selemat jalan!* (Happy traveling!)

Unity in
Diversity

R EACHING ACROSS THE SPARKLING BLUE WATERS, INDO-
nesia appears enchanting and lovely. Unlike most countries,
Indonesia is not one solid land mass. Instead, it is the largest
archipelago in the world. Because of its size, it is still the fourteenth largest country on the planet. The Indonesians refer to
it as *Tanah Air Kita*, Our Earth and Water, and their national
motto is "unity in diversity." All of the islands are sprinkled
over an area of 741,097 square miles (1,919,440 square kilometers), ranging in size from uninhabited specks, to huge
islands that are home to millions. While most geographers
estimate Indonesia at 13,677 islands, recent satellite pictures
have pushed the estimate to more than 18,000. If you were to
travel to a different island each day, it could take you up to
fifty years to see them all.

Water, Water Everywhere

Oceans and seas surround Indonesia on all sides. Water covers
35,900 square miles (93,000 sq km) of the country's total area.
The Pacific and Indian Oceans border part of the islands,
while seas such as Andaman and Flores link island groups.
The islands themselves contain countless beautiful freshwater
lakes (*danau*) and rivers (*sungai*).

On some islands, such as Kalimantan, rivers are the highways that transport people from one place to another. The
capital city is named Banjarmasin, but is officially nicknamed

Opposite: **A portion of Indonesia's thousands of islands can be seen in this satellite image.**

"River City." Floating homes there are made out of wood, and even the markets float on the water! Visitors to River City are sometimes taught how to build their own bamboo rafts and how to use a pole to push them down the river. The more adventurous travelers may take a trip down the river's white-water rapids that challenge even the most trained guides.

In Banjarmasin many of the homes are built on stilts over water.

The busiest river in Kalimantan is the Mahakam River. Riverboats cross it many times a day, taking people to and from work. For quicker trips, some people board motorized canoes. Some of the currents in this river are so swift and lethal that even the locals avoid them.

The lakes, or *danau*, of Indonesia are especially beautiful. Many are cradled in what was once a volcano, and their deep blue waters reflect breathtaking mountain ranges on all sides. In Sulawesi, Lake Tempe is a temperamental body of water. During the island's wet season, the lake runs high, often breaking out across its boundaries and flooding homes. Even though most are on stilts, many families must still grab their belongings and move quickly to avoid the water's power. In the dry season, Lake Tempe can completely dry up and become nothing but a large, sandy bowl. The people of the island walk across it or travel in horse-drawn carriages from one side to the other.

Danu Batur, on the island of Bali, is a smaller lake, measuring a mere 6.2 miles (10 km) in diameter. It makes up for its size in beauty, however, with a temple dedicated to the

The Mahakam River is wide and deep in some areas while other parts are roaring rapids.

The Day the Earth Shook

It was a quiet morning on December 26, 2004, when suddenly, the ground shook with the tremendous power of a 9.0 magnitude earthquake. It was so powerful that scientists say it slightly affected the earth's rotation, causing it to wobble just a bit on its axis. The epicenter of the quake was a mere 100 miles (160 km) from the western coast of Sumatra. This quake was the fourth largest in recorded history, and it brought great destruction. The devastation did not end when the ground stopped shaking, however.

Deep under the ocean waters, tectonic plates shifted violently, and a tsunami (a huge sea wave) was born. Just minutes after the quake, the tsunami, reported to be upward of 50 feet (15 meters) tall, hit many parts of Asia. By the time it was over, the death toll stood at more than 155,000. Over 100,000 were Indonesians. The Indonesian ambassador to Malaysia stated that he believed that number would eventually reach 400,000.

Almost 125,000 are still missing and 500,000 are without homes. Hundreds of villages along the coast of Sumatra completely disappeared. Roads and bridges were gone. The province of Aceh was particularly hard hit. Most of its homes and businesses were completely flattened (above).

A number of other countries, such as Sri Lanka and India, were also horrifically damaged during this natural disaster. Experts estimate that altogether at least 1.5 million people were killed, injured, gone missing, or became homeless.

After the disaster occurred, thousands of volunteers from all over the world flew in to help the Indonesians. Many countries, including the United States, pledged millions of dollars for relief efforts, and donations poured in from all points on the globe. Telethons were held to raise money to help victims begin to recover from one of history's biggest natural disasters.

Goddess of the Lake on one rim. The hot springs at the edge often reach temperatures of 135 degrees Fahrenheit (57 degrees Celsius).

Perhaps the most beautiful lake in all of Indonesia is Lake Toba in northern Sumatra. Like many of the bodies of water in this country, it was first formed when a volcano erupted over 75,000 years ago. The explosion was so big that the sides of the crater fell inward and created a huge cauldron-shaped hole that filled with water. It was more than 56 miles (90 km) long and 19 miles (31 km) wide. The land was not done shifting, however, and 30,000 years later, it shook again. The base

Northern Sumatra is home to one of the world's largest crater lakes, Toba.

of the crater split in half, and the pieces of the volcano's sides crashed into the water. Today, two of the largest pieces can still be seen sticking up above the water. The one on the northeast side made a peninsula, while the one in the middle created Samosir, or the Isle of the Dead. At 1,661 feet (505 m), Toba is one of the world's deepest lakes. On the north side, a 360-foot (110-m) waterfall, called Sipiso-piso, draws countless visitors.

The island of Flores contains three of the most spectacular lakes found in Indonesia. Like other lakes, they sit in the craters of dormant volcanoes, but these three have something unique. They are located near each other; only low ridges separate them. Despite their geographic closeness, they have distinctly different colors. One is deep blue; the next is bright turquoise; and the third is dark burgundy. Quite unpredictably,

The dormant volcano of Keli Mutu has three lakes, each exhibiting a different color. Two can be seen in this photo.

they will even shift colors! Scientists suspect that this is due to the minerals in the water. As the minerals dissolve, the water makes its way into deeper layers and the acidity of the water is altered, thus changing its color. Natives have a much more spiritual theory. They believe the colors change because one lake houses the souls of sinners; one, the souls of sorcerers; and the third, the souls of innocent infants and virgins.

Land, Ho!

Although Indonesia is mainly made of water, its many islands are rich and diverse. At a mere 15 million years old, they are also quite young on the geological timeline. The islands form a slightly curved shape much like a crescent moon in the middle of blue water. The country is bordered by East Timor, Malaysia, Papua New Guinea, Brunei, Singapore, and Australia.

While Indonesia consists of thousands of islands, many of them are only a mile or two wide and home to nothing more than some trees, plants, and the occasional bird. From the sky, they are either invisible or just a tiny dot of color against endless blue. Other islands are huge, with millions of people. Java, although not a huge island, contains 100 million people. Kalimantan is much larger but has fewer people, especially in the interior. Among the thousands of islands, most people are found on the Greater and Lesser Sunda Islands, as well as the Maluku Islands and Papua New Guinea.

The Greater Sunda Islands consist of Sumatra, Java, Kalimantan, and Sulawesi. The majority of the country's

Mountains frame vibrant green rice fields in Sumatra.

population lives here. Sumatra is Indonesia's third largest island and the sixth largest in the world. It is the country's most western island and is roughly the size of Spain. Approximately 37 million people live there. It is a land so rich in natural scenery that it is hard to take them all in. Shimmering lakes, towering volcanoes, bright green rice fields, and rambling tobacco plantations can all be found there.

Java is considered the heart of Indonesia and is just about the size of New York. It is the country's most developed island and is the center for culture, politics, and economics. More than 107 million people live here, making up almost half of the country's entire population. Jakarta is a bustling city full of the sounds of loud music, the calls of street vendors, the laughter of children, and the din of unending traffic. It has some of the most fertile soil in all the islands, thanks to the ash from its many active volcanoes.

The island of Borneo is split between two nations. Two-thirds of the island belong to Indonesia; the rest belong to Malaysia. The Indonesian half of the island is called Kalimantan. Almost 10 million people live there. Parts of it are still very beautiful with waterways for roads, but a growing amount of the land is being filled up with oil refineries and timber mills.

Sulawesi is the last of the Greater Sunda Islands. It is a little smaller than Great Britain. It is shaped quite oddly, like an octopus with four tentacles. The 13 million people on Sulawesi have learned to live with rugged terrain since the island has large mountains, deep valleys, and almost a dozen active volcanoes.

A hilltop view of Sulawasi's mountains and valleys.

Taking a Look at Indonesia's Cities

With 6,000 inhabited islands, the number of cities and provinces in Indonesia is almost infinite. Denpasar (below), is the capital of Bali, located on the island's southern point. Its name means "next to the market." The name fits well, as it is a city full of endless rows of shops. Over the last twenty-five years it has experienced a great deal of development. The city's population tripled between 1970 and 1990, and today more than 360,000 people live there. The majority are Javanese workers. The city's income is largely based on

tourism, and it is the site of the international airport. Tourists may stop to walk through the Bali Provincial State Museum or the cultural arts center, Taman Werdhi Budaya, but few stay in Denpasar for long. The traffic and noise make it too hectic to enjoy.

Medan is the capital of North Sumatra and the third largest city in Indonesia, with a population of more than 2.5 million. It is the primary place for tourists to enter and exit Indonesia since it has both a large harbor and an airport. Like Denpasar, visitors pass through the city quickly to avoid overcrowding and pollution.

The capital city of West Sumatra is Padang. This bustling area is the main place for trading spices and other goods like rubber, cinnamon, coffee, tea, and nutmeg (above). Almost 700,000 people live there. The city has a Kampung Cina, or Chinatown, where visitors can stroll through Chinese businesses, coffee shops, and turn-of-the-century homes. Tourists can also see a 140-year-old home that doubles as a museum. It features traditional wedding and dance costumes, musical instruments, and even weapons.

The Lesser Sunda Islands run from Bali to Timor and include the islands of Lombok, Sumbawa, Sumba, and Flores. Here the islands are much smaller and, due to their geology, drier. Bali has over 3 million people, however, and is a well-known vacation spot for many tourists. Timor is divided in half. The eastern half declared its independence from Indonesia in 1999, becoming the nation of East Timor.

The Maluku Islands number more than 1,000 and are called the Spice Islands. Fewer than 2 million people live throughout this region, and many of them are still living in tribal communities, following unique traditions and customs. The capital is Ambon, with a population of 250,000. It was once the world's center for cloves, and today it is still an important trading spot.

Last in the Indonesian archipelago is the huge island of New Guinea. A portion of New Guinea belongs to the nation of Papua; the rest is called Irian Jaya and belongs to Indonesia. Wilderness is supreme here, with everything from mangrove swamps to mountains covered in snow. Indonesia's highest peak, Puncak Jaya ("Victory Peak"), is found there, rising 16,503 feet (5,030 km) into the sky. There are very few roads between towns, and while boats can take people from place to place, they are not reliable.

Irian Jaya, Indonesia's largest province, can be found in the western side of the island of New Guinea.

A Land of Volcanoes

For the people of Indonesia, erupting volcanoes and trembling ground are familiar events. Their islands were originally created by the shifting of Earth's plates and volcanic eruptions, and that activity continues to plague the islands. Indonesia is part of the "Ring of Fire," a line of volcanoes that strings along the Pacific Ocean. Indonesia has more than 500 volcanoes, 129 of which are considered active. Smoke rises from their cone-shaped tops, and at least one explodes nearly every year. Mount Merapi, near the city of Yogyakarta, is considered one of the most dangerous volcanoes. As recently as June 2004, several people were killed when a volcano in East Java erupted unexpectedly. Small earthquakes and tremors shake the ground somewhere in Indonesia every single day. In November 2004, two quakes hit West Papua and Alor Island, killing more than a dozen people and destroying hundreds of homes and

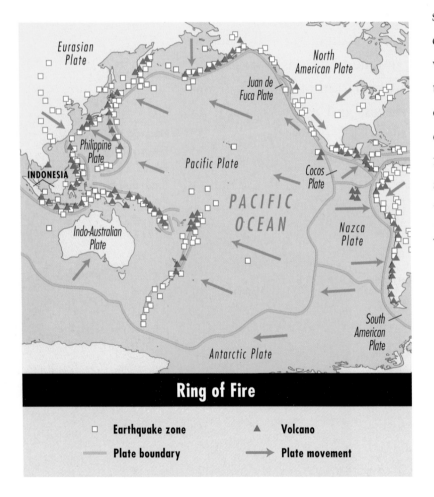

Ring of Fire

□ Earthquake zone	▲ Volcano
— Plate boundary	→ Plate movement

A Big Bang

The volcanic island of Krakatoa (sometimes spelled Krakatau) used to be between Java and Sumatra. In May 1883, a violent earthquake shook the island. Tremors continued for three months. Then, on August 26 and 27, there were four tremendous explosions over a five-hour period. These eruptions were so large that geographers estimate they were equivalent to a 100-megaton nuclear bomb. The 2,600-foot (793-m) tall mountain was gone, and in its place was a hole in the ocean floor 1,000 feet (305 m) deep.

The eruption of Krakatoa was one of the most devastating in history. On Java and Sumatra, more than 165 villages were destroyed and 36,000 people were killed, many of them by tsunamis that towered 115 feet (35 m) high. These tidal waves spread through the surrounding waters, sinking dozens of ships at Calcutta, India, 2,000 miles (3,200 km) away. Hundreds of ships in harbors such as Port Elizabeth, South Africa 5,000 miles (8,000 km) away, were damaged. The blast was heard 3,000 miles (4,800 km) away!

For almost three days after the eruption, the skies above Java and Sumatra were pitch black. The sun, moon, and stars were invisible. Dust from the explosion caused spectacular sunsets around the world for three years.

For the people throughout the islands, the explosion represented a sign of the imbalance in nature—and foretold that kingdoms were about to gain new leaders, who would calm and stabilize the realm and, indirectly, the land. Today, at the site of Krakatoa are the beginnings of another volcano, referred to as *Anak Krakatau*, or Son of Krakatoa. It is already rumbling and hissing quietly and remains a site of great superstition, as some Indonesians believe the devil lives there still.

other buildings. While volcanic activity sometimes result in tragedy, the ash helps to make some of Indonesia's soil some of the richest and most fertile in the world.

Very Wet and Less Wet

Indonesia lies in what is called the equatorial ever-wet zone, another way of saying hot and humid! Unlike many other parts of the world, this country does not have four distinct seasons of fall, winter, spring, and summer. Instead, it has a wet and a dry season, and each one lasts about six months. The wet season, often called the monsoon, lasts from November to March, with most of the rain falling in December and January. The lowland areas average between 51 and 71 inches (130 to 180 centimeters) of rain, while the mountainous regions get as much as 177 inches (450 cm). During this season, it is not unusual for parts of Sumatra, Java, and Kalimantan to be completely flooded.

Indonesia's more than 500 volcanoes make it one of the world's most volcanic countries.

On some of the wettest islands, rain forest treetops soar over 130 feet (40 m) into the sky. Their branches grow together, creating nature's own green canopy roof.

The dry season lasts from June to October. It rains less, although the temperature remains warm and the humidity never drops below 75 percent. Forests begin to turn brown, and fires are common. Temperatures in Indonesia vary depending on location. Along the coast, the temperature stays around 80°F (27°C) all year long. In the highlands, it ranges from 68°F to 70°F (20 to 21°C). Despite the heat and rain, several mountains are covered with snow year-round.

Indonesia's Geographic Features

Highest Elevation: Puncak Jaya, 16,503 feet (5,030 m)

Lowest Elevation: Sea level

Greatest Distance North to South: 1,200 miles (1,930 km)

Greatest Distance East to West: 3,200 miles (5,150 km)

Longest River: Kapuas in Kalimantan, 700 miles (1,126 km)

Largest Lake: Toba in Sumatra, 426 square miles (1,103 sq km)

Longest Mountain Chain: Sudirman Range in West Papua, 311 miles (500 km)

Largest City (2003 est.): Jakarta in Java, 8,827,900 people

Highest Average Temperature: 80°F (27°C) in coastal areas

Lowest Average Temperature: 70°F (21°C) in the highlands

A Wildlife Treasure Trove

N 1854, A WILDLIFE NATURALIST NAMED SIR ALFRED RUSSEL Wallace started on an eight-year journey throughout the islands of Indonesia. His job was one many would envy. He traveled the world gathering wildlife specimens for various museums. While he was in Indonesia, he managed to collect 125,000 types of flora and fauna. In the process, he discovered something about the chain of islands that no one had ever noted before. He realized that Indonesia was actually two separate zones when it came to plants and animals. In his opinion, there was a distinct division between the two. This line, now called the Wallace Line, runs along the edge of the Sunda shelf between Kalimantan and Sulawesi and south through the strait between Bali and Lombok. On the east side of the line, the wildlife resembles the nature of Australia, while on the west side, it is similar to Asia's. A few of the islands, including Sulawesi and Maluku, are sometimes referred to as Wallacea, transitional islands where the two types of wildlife seem to merge.

Opposite: **The Sumatran tiger is found only in Sumatra. It is estimated that there are only five hundred of them left in the wild.**

The moth orchid is one of the many varieties found in Indonesia.

From Orchids to Banyan Trees

Among the thousands of islands that make up the country of Indonesia are almost more flowers than anyone could count. Upward of 40,000 species are

Rafflesia, the Super Flower

Although Indonesia has three national flowers (jasmine, moon orchid, and rafflesia), it is clear which one tops the list. *Rafflesia arnoldi* is the world's largest and heaviest flower, often reaching 3.28 feet (1 m) in diameter and weighing up to 19.8 pounds (9 kilograms). It has no leaves, stems, or roots, but rather obtains its nutrients from the plants it grows on. Like most flowers, rafflesia has a scent to it, but it is not something anyone would want in a vase on the kitchen table. This flower smells like rotting meat, and while most people would not care for that, many insects find it irresistible. They fly to it and pollinate it in the process. They have to hurry, though, because this unusual flower only blooms when it is ready to reproduce. The blooms only last a few days. Rafflesia can be found only in special forests and parks in Borneo, Sumatra, and Java.

found there, making up 10 percent of all the world's species. Among them are 5,000 kinds of orchids, from the huge tiger orchid to the tiny, leafless *taeniophyllum*.

A great deal of Indonesia is made up of rich, fertile rain forests. They feature everything from tall, graceful trees to carpets of moss, with vines, ferns, and bushes in between. The flora of Indonesia includes a huge variety of trees. The lowlands have the most species. Kalimantan has 3,000 different

kinds alone. These include hundreds of acres of mangroves, unusual trees that grow in salt water and swamps and provide shelter for many birds and fish. The sacred banyan, a type of fig tree, is also found here. It has branches that grow back down to the ground and root, creating a vaultlike area under the tree that some natives use for religious ceremonies.

The flora of the highlands grows much more slowly than in the lowlands, and there are fewer species found there. Chestnut, laurel, sandalwood, ebony, and oak trees grow in thick forests, and wide alpine meadows dot the land. Spice trees like clove and nutmeg grow there also.

Highly prized trees grow in the rain forests of Indonesia. Illegal logging and deforestation threaten this natural habitat.

Although Indonesia is rich with thick rain forests and countless, colorful riots of blooms, it has also struggled with terrible fires. In 1997 and 1998, fires raged through East Kalimantan forests for weeks on end, thanks to a drought and to various national and international companies cutting down the rain forests. As the trees disappeared, no new ones were planted, leaving a base of dried leaves and grasses, the perfect tinder for uncontrollable fires. Some scientists consider the Indonesian fires to be one of history's greatest ecological disasters. Over 12.8 million acres (5.2 million hectares) were destroyed, and the smog and smoke spread out across 1,000 miles (1,609 km), creating a gray haze over many of Indonesia's islands, as well as Malaysia, Thailand, the Philippines, and Singapore. The pollution contaminated water supplies, sickened people, and drastically reduced tourism.

In recent years, Indonesia has begun to focus more on environmental issues such as the continuing loss of its rain forests. A growing number of Indonesian environmental nongovernmental organizations have been working not only to address the ongoing issue of deforestation, but also to preserve the unique habitats of the region's wildlife. The country has now set aside 6 percent of its land to be used as nature reserves and national parks in order to protect its flora and fauna.

Drought and logging contributed to fires in Kalimantan forests, destroying over 12 million acres of forestland.

The Animals of Indonesia

Many of the more unusual animals found in Indonesia can be found only in Indonesia. The *babi rusa*, or deerlike pig, is one of them. It has long, curved tusks that come out of the side of its mouth and go right through the top of its snout. Other indigenous creatures include the *anoa*, or dwarf buffalo, which looks like a cross between a cow and a deer, and *musang*, or weasel-like civet cat. The *binatang hantu*, or "spooky animal," is an animal similar to a lemur, with long, clingy fingers. Geckos are found on many islands, running up trees and walls and often entertaining tourists as they hunt for mosquitoes to munch.

Other animals include the rarely seen leopard and blue panther, as well as the almost extinct Sumatran tiger. The *badak jawa* is an endangered one-horned rhinoceros that can only be found in the nation's parks. Tiny mouse deer live in the thickest parts of the forests. Although they look like deer, they only stand 18 to 22 inches (46 to 56 cm) tall.

The very small mouse deer makes its home in the forests of Indonesia.

On the eastern islands, marsupials similar to those in Australia can be spotted in the wild, including tree-climbing kangaroos and rabbitlike, nocturnal bandicoots. The bizarre-

Armorlike scales cover the pangolin from the tip of its nose to the tip of its tail.

looking pangolin also lives on these islands. It has a long tail and is covered with big, flat scales, much like the armadillo. It sleeps during the day and comes out at night. When frightened, it curls up into a ball; its name means "rolling over."

Indonesia's islands contain many primates, including gibbons, macaques, proboscis monkeys, and orangutans. The orangutans—named from Malay *orang*, person, and *utan*, forest—live in Kalimantan and Sumatra. They cannot be found anywhere else in the world outside of zoos. These unusual animals remind many of humans and are able to walk on their hind legs, although they spend most of their time swinging from branch to branch with their long, strong arms.

Orangutans are endangered and so are protected at both the Orangutan Viewing Centre in North Sumatra and the Tanjung Puting National Park. They can also be found in a special rehabilitation center at Gunung Leuser National Park.

These orangutans in Tanjung Puting National Park are well protected.

A Less and Less Familiar Face

In the past, the expressive face of the black macaque monkey was a familiar one in the Indonesian rain forests. Ranging in size from 19 to 26 inches (48 to 66 cm), the macaque has brown or black fur, cream-colored tufts on its cheeks, and a large, off-white patch on its rump. They are fruit eaters and often stuff an entire piece of fruit in their mouths as they walk. Chewing the pulp, they spit out the seeds as they go, spreading seeds from place to place throughout the forest. In recent years, the number of macaque monkeys has steadily decreased. According to wildlife conservationists, the reason is clear. Black macaque monkeys in Indonesia are equivalent to turkeys in the United States. They are found less often in the rain forests and more often on the dinner table. Currently studies are underway to help increase the number of these creatures before they disappear completely.

Some animals that do not actually have wings seem to be able to fly from tree to tree thanks to membranes on their legs that act like built-in hang gliders. Flying lemurs, squirrels, lizards, and bats soar across the gaps between treetops. Even the paradise snake throws its body from place to place, curling into a U-shape and whipping through the air.

The grounds of the rain forests are often alive with colored and varied insects. There are fluttering luna moths, large atlas beetles, and giant walking sticks that sometimes reach 8 inches (20 cm) in length. Many of Indonesia's insects are hard to see, as they are excellent examples of natural camouflage. Walking sticks seem to melt into a pile of leaves on the forest floor, while horned toads sit quietly in a pile of torn leaves. Leaf insects sway in the breeze, and katydids pose in threatening positions to look like a wasp.

Indonesia's rain forests are alive with insects. Some are difficult to spot, like this giant walking stick.

Indonesia's wetlands attract many species of birds, including the egret.

More than 1,500 species of birds live in Indonesia, including 400 that are found only there. Egrets, herons, hawks, and eagles nest there, as well as the *rangkong enggang*, or hornbill, with its huge, horn-tipped beak. On Irian Jaya and Maluku, large, flightless cassowaries share the land with more than forty species of vibrantly colored birds of paradise and parrots.

Return of the Dinosaur?

It looks like a long-lost relative of the dinosaurs or dragons. When it was first spotted in 1910 on the coast of Komodo, some thought a lost cousin to the huge lizards had been found. They were partially right. It was the largest known lizard in the world. The Komodo has been known to reach 10 feet (3 m) in length and weigh up to 330 pounds (150 kg). A powerful reptile, it can move as fast as 18.6 miles per hour (30 kph) as it tracks down its next meal. It has a very sharp sense of smell with a range of up to 1 mile (1.6 km). With its sharp claws, twenty-six notched teeth, and jaws that open wide for large prey, the meat-eating Komodo is a truly frightening sight. It rarely ever hurts a human, however, and has recently been named Indonesia's national animal.

Treasure from Under the Water

It is not too surprising that the world turns to Indonesia to import exotic and ornamental fish for aquariums, since its waters contains one-quarter of the world's entire fish species. With all of its lakes, rivers, seas, and oceans, the choices are almost limitless. Some of the most popular types of fish exported are the colorful clownfish, sea horses, and yellow, black, and white bannerfish.

The ocean waters are also alive with poisonous sea snakes, sharks, and starfish. Beds of coral line the ocean's floors, as

barracudas and manta rays swim quietly by. Now and then visitors catch a glimpse of playful dolphins. Giant sea turtles are found in the ocean and on the beaches, but theirs is a life full of risk. Their numbers have been dropping because they are frequently hunted by locals to put on the dinner table as part of the meal. Burying their eggs under the sand of beaches is dangerous too, since tourists and other people occasionally get in the way or try to interfere. In response to this, a number of the national parks throughout Java and Bali offer safe places for sea turtles to lay their eggs. They also encourage natives not to eat turtle meat so that the flagging turtle populations have a chance to recover and grow.

The wildlife of Indonesia is as wild and varied as the islands themselves. From the mangroves' looping roots to the orangutans' reddish-orange hair, there are sights to delight the senses and ignite the imagination of tourists and natives alike.

The coral reefs off Indonesia's shores are full of vibrantly colored fish.

The Cradle of Mankind

INDONESIA'S RICH AND LONG HISTORY REACHES BACK ALMOST a half-million years. The islands were once home to *Homo erectus*, whose fragile fossils were found there only 100 years ago. Later, hundreds of kingdoms were scattered across the archipelago, resulting in a wonderful variety of customs, art, and cultures. Invasions were common. The Portuguese came in the early 1500s, searching for spices, followed by the Dutch, who fought many wars on Java. In 1811, Britain briefly was in power, and then the islands returned to Dutch rule. Finally, Japan invaded in 1941. It was not until 1945 that Indonesia declared its independence, and slowly begin to create its own identity as a new nation and republic.

Opposite: **Indonesia's history includes a wealth of customs and cultures left by the various peoples of the islands.**

The reconstructed face of Java Man confirmed life in Indonesia dating back five hundred thousand years.

A Prehistory Discovered

In 1891, a Dutch military doctor named Eugene Dubois made an important discovery in Java. He found a fossil of an early human's jawbone that dated back 500,000 years. It was nicknamed the "Java Man." Experts reconstructed the face from the skull and found that this form of *Homo erectus* had large brow ridges, a jutting jaw, and a small chin.

Archaeologists believe that these early humans did not have the ability to speak but could communicate with grunts and gestures. They could use crude stone tools and usually lived in caves. In 1936, additional fossils were found in the same area that dated back 1 million years.

In 2004, explorers in a cave on Flores came upon a skeleton of a different type. These humans lived 18,000 to 80,000 years ago and stood 3 feet (1 m) tall, about the size of the average three-year-old. Experts named it *Homo floresiensis* in honor of where it was found. They will be studying these remains for years to come. All of these prehistoric finds showed scholars that Southeast Asia truly was the cradle, or birthplace, for much of mankind.

Approximately 30,000 to 40,000 years ago, a group of people called *Pygmy negritos* lived on some of Indonesia's islands. They were small people with dark, wool-like hair. They were joined centuries later by humans known as *Australoids*. These people were able to create and use a number of tools and even had their own art. Their stenciled handprints, dating back 20,000 to 60,000 years, were found in a cave in Kalimantan in 1999, as well as in caves on Sulawesi and Papua.

The years between 3000 and 500 B.C. were an era of migration, as people shifted from one land to another. A third group of people, known as *Austronesians*, arrived in Indonesia from northern Indochina. They brought with them the knowledge of cultivating crops and raising livestock. It was not long before they had displaced the other tribes of people to interior forests. They took over the most fertile lands and created

A Timeline of Kingdoms

3,000–500 B.C.	Austronesians
2nd century B.C.	Indianized kingdoms
7th–3rd centuries B.C.	Buddhist kingdom of Srivijaya and Mataram
13th–16th centuries	Majapahit and the Golden Age of Indonesia
17th–18th centuries	Dutch East India
19th century to present	Nationalist Party

communal, or village, living. New planting methods such as wet-rice cultivation were introduced. This technique involved raising seedlings in nursery beds, transferring them to a paddy, or flooded field, and then letting them grow until harvesttime.

Another Culture's Influence

In the second century, civilizations began to appear that were based on Indic culture. The architecture, politics, and government modeled India's, but how Southeast Asia knew so much about that faraway culture still puzzles some historians. There are two possibilities. First, a number of students were sent by boat to India to learn about its lifestyle and then returned to share that knowledge. Others think that Indian Brahman

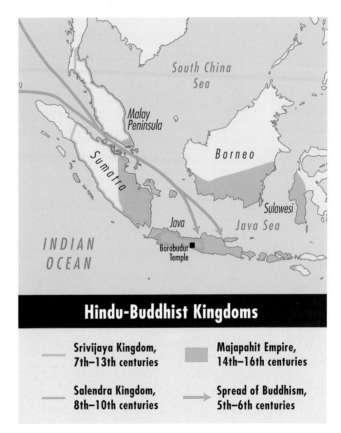

Hindu-Buddhist Kingdoms

Srivijaya Kingdom, 7th–13th centuries	Majapahit Empire, 14th–16th centuries
Salendra Kingdom, 8th–10th centuries	Spread of Buddhism, 5th–6th centuries

priests traveled to the kingdom to teach the Southeast Asian people about Indic culture.

The rulers of these early Indic kingdoms were seen as divine—the actual reincarnation of Hindu gods—and thus had limitless ability to do whatever they wanted. This meant that they had great power, status, and wealth.

These Indianized kingdoms relied on the seas surrounding them for trade. Sailors spent more time on board a ship than on land. Some of the world's largest ships were found in their harbors. A strong trading system was established throughout the Indian Ocean and as far away as Rome and Persia. Spices were exported, and knowledge and skills like textile dyeing, sculpting, and astronomy were brought back in return.

These kingdoms flourished for centuries. In the seventh century, a Buddhist kingdom called Srivijaya emerged. Centered in Sumatra, its entire culture also was based on the sea and the trade it provided. Merchants came from Persia, India, and Arabia, and everything from spices to silks were traded for wood and precious gems. Some of the traders also brought a new religion to Sumatra, Java, and other islands: Islam. When explorer Marco Polo visited the kingdom in 1292, he wrote of seeing Muslims there. Islam spread along the trade routes. Local leaders and residents were attracted to mosques, or Islamic churches, by the exciting *gamelan* music played there. While they were inside listening to the music, they were introduced to the tenets of the religion and strongly urged to convert to it.

A Famous Traveler

One of history's best-known travelers was Italian Marco Polo. From an early age, Polo accompanied his father and uncle on their frequent business trips. While he was in China, he served as Kublai Khan's agent and as governor of the Chinese city of Yangchow. During his five-month stay in Srivijaya, he noted the influence of the Islamic religion as it began to spread across Indonesia.

Polo's life was full of adventures, and much of what he saw, he wrote about in his book, *The Travels of Marco Polo*. Despite all of the memories he shared of his discoveries, his last words upon his death in 1324 were, "I did not tell half of what I saw."

The Golden Age Begins

By 1300, the trading and cultural center of Indonesia was in east Java in a kingdom named Majapahit. It received gifts and tributes from places as far away as the coast of Malay Peninsula. The king and his elaborate parades visited many areas in order to receive these treasures.

The kingdom was a center for both rice agriculture and far-flung trade. Canals brought boats and goods inland from the coast. Red brick temples with split gates (no top or bottom pieces, like western saloon doors) were built everywhere. Performance art and culture flourished, and many Indian epics like the Ramayana were told with Javanese characters. The poet Prapanca called this time period the Golden Age.

Beginning in 1300, some local leaders from coastal towns and inland kingdoms began to convert to the new religion, Islam. Traders who became Muslims strengthened their ties

Bronze statue of Buddha from the Majapahit dynasty

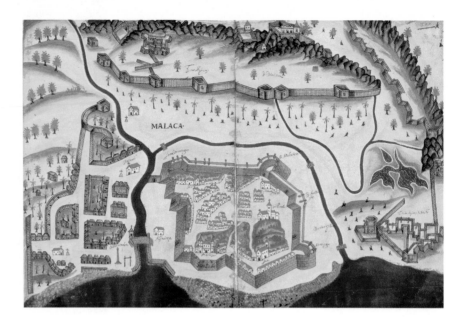

Malacca, an important trading port on the Malay Peninsula, was the center of Islamic trade. Islam was adopted by many traders and brought back to Indonesia.

to the new port city of Malacca, an important port on the Malay Peninsula where Singapore is located today. This port became the center of Islamic trade in Asia. Islam spread from the local leaders to the common people. This new religion valued equality among its members. Today, 88 percent of all Indonesians are Muslim.

The traders and the people of the coastal town settlements began to challenge the old Hindu kings for rule of Java. When Majapahit fell in 1527, a new kingdom called Mataram in south-central Java replaced it. The rise of Islam had affected the area not only religiously but also politically. By the end of the fifteenth century, it was considered the state religion. Arab and Persian traders continued to support local kingdoms but not empires. Several small Muslim states developed, and each one of their rulers declared himself a sultan. These were the Indonesians who faced the Europeans, the next wave of visitors to Southeast Asia.

Portuguese explorers arrived in Indonesia in the late fifteenth century seeking spices.

The Arrival of the Europeans

The first Europeans to set foot in Indonesia were the Portuguese in the late 1400s. They came to get spices for trading and remained for more than a century. Word of the riches they found spread quickly. Spices were in high demand at this time. Without refrigeration, food spoiled, and spices helped not only to make it last longer but also to disguise the taste of spoiling. Europeans happily paid great sums for the spices found throughout Indonesia. It was not long before other explorers began to travel to the

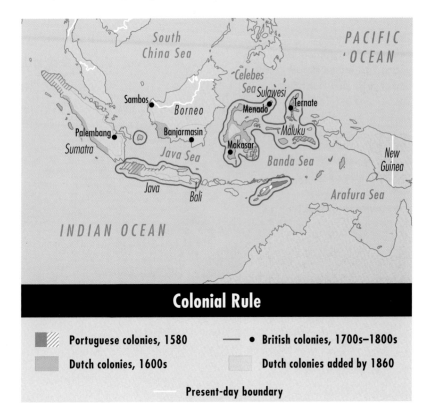

South China Sea

PACIFIC OCEAN

Sambos
Borneo
Celebes Sea Sulawesi
Menado
Ternate
Palembang
Banjarmasin
Maluku
Sumatra
Makasar
Java Sea
Banda Sea
New Guinea
Java
Bali
Arafura Sea

INDIAN OCEAN

Colonial Rule

◩ Portuguese colonies, 1580 — ● British colonies, 1700s–1800s

▨ Dutch colonies, 1600s   Dutch colonies added by 1860

— Present-day boundary

The Dutch controlled Indonesia for two hundred years. This native statue depicts a seated Dutchman.

The Dutch East India Company not only sold spices, it also operated such colonial activities as organizing armies for the Dutch.

islands too. One of the biggest groups to visit was the Dutch. Once they arrived, they remained.

Led by an accountant named Jan Pieterszoon Coen, the Dutch took over the Javanese kingdom of Jayakarta and renamed it Batavia. It was a violent takeover. Ships that were not from Holland were immediately sunk as they approached the harbor. Entire islands were captured for use as spice plantations, and thousands of natives were killed so Dutch workers could take their land. By the end of the seventeenth century, the Dutch controlled all of the spice, coffee, sugar, pepper, tea, and cotton production.

To keep everything organized, the Dutch formed the Dutch East India Company, with headquarters in Batavia. This powerful business kept track of the enormous profits

being generated by the sale of spices. It also created and negotiated treaties and raised armies in order to wage wars on Holland's behalf. For the next two centuries, the Dutch continued to expand their control over Indonesia, renaming it the Dutch East Indies.

Although the Dutch were quite pleased with how everything was going, the people of Sumatra and Java began to fight against Dutch domination. Because all of their time was spent on growing crops for Holland, there was little time left over to grow enough food for their own families. Many were starving, and unrest was growing steadily. Although they continually lost, the military cost to keep them under control took a significant toll on the Dutch East India Company. In 1799, they went bankrupt. Holland stepped in and created a colony known as Netherlands East Indies.

When Britain took control of the Dutch colonies, Sir Thomas Stamford Raffles, as governor, made reforms to better life on Java.

Holland, though, was struggling. France had invaded it in 1795, and then from 1811 to 1815, Indonesia was lost to the British. Under the governorship of Sir Thomas Stamford Raffles, Java saw a number of changes. Raffles worked to end the forced labor of Indonesian people and gave them more choices in what crops to grow. In 1816, after Napoleon was defeated and France left Holland, the Dutch

A Rebel of Her Time

One voice that made a difference for many Indonesians was Raden Ajeng Kartini's (1879–1904). The daughter of a Javanese aristocrat, she was deeply concerned about the lack of education her people were given, especially women. She founded a school for women in north-central Java and, toward the end of her life, wrote a number of letters to friends in Holland about how badly the Indonesian people were treated. The letters were published after her death in *Door Duisternis Tot Licht*, or "From Darkness to Light."

regained control of the islands. Nothing had changed, and they continued to treat the people cruelly. They kept building plantations that caused locals to starve. In 1825, a Javanese prince named Diponegoro had had enough. He began what would be known as the Java War. It was only one of many peasant uprisings, but it showed that a local leader could fight against foreign domination. It lasted for five years, and before it was over, more than 200,000 Javanese and 8,000 Dutch died, primarily because of starvation and disease. Although Diponegoro was arrested during the peace negotiations, he is still considered one of Indonesia's greatest heroes and is often referred to as the "Just Prince." He died in exile at the age of seventy.

The Dutch refused to educate the natives. Only a very elite few, usually from Java and Sumatra, were allowed western schooling. Those that were educated began to desire independence. They formed political groups. In 1927, the Nationalist Party was created under the leadership of a Javanese named Sukarno. A gifted speaker and passionate leader, he spearheaded the demand for independence from the Dutch, and soon the islands were filled with the youthful

Indonesian statesman, Achmed Sukarno, visits his people.

pledge of "One People, One Language, One Nation." In 1930, Sukarno was exiled for his actions.

Japanese soldiers raised their flag in Java as they took control of Indonesia in the early 1940s.

Under Japanese Control

Just after their attack on Pearl Harbor in World War II, Japan invaded Indonesia. They were welcomed with open arms. Although the Japanese were there in hopes of getting the fuel they needed for their planes, the Indonesians hoped they were there to liberate them from the Dutch. In the beginning, it seemed as if this might happen. Sukarno and other leaders forced into exile were released, but freedom ended there. The Japanese brought more misery. For more than three years, they forced the Indonesians to work as slaves producing the rice they needed. All crops were sent to Japan, and soon Indonesians were starving again.

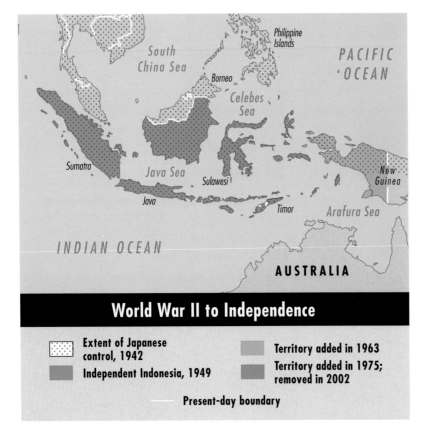

World War II to Independence

- Extent of Japanese control, 1942
- Independent Indonesia, 1949
- Territory added in 1963
- Territory added in 1975; removed in 2002
- Present-day boundary

On August 15, 1945, Japan surrendered, ending their control in Indonesia. Two days later, Sukarno declared the country's independence. Once more, the Dutch tried to step in and take over the land they knew so well. It took four years of guerilla fighting and pressure from the United Nations before they finally stopped. Soon after, Sukarno became the first president of this new nation.

Independence and Instability

Even though the country was finally free of Dutch control, it was still in turmoil as 169 different political parties fought for leadership. The government was stalemated throughout the 1950s. Sukarno focused on uniting the islands and creating the concept of one nation. In 1956, he created a "guided democracy," which gave much decision-making power to the president. Three years later, regional and factional problems caused him to begin acting as the country's dictator. In 1963, he proclaimed he was Indonesia's Supreme Ruler for life.

In 1965 students in Jakarta demonstrate against Communism in Indonesia.

General Suharto became leader of Indonesia replacing Sukarno.

Many Indonesians were unhappy, especially when it became clear that Sukarno was spending the country's money in ways that some of the people thought unfair. While the people lived in poverty, he lived in luxury. Money that could have gone for education and health care was instead spent on building sports stadiums and monuments. In addition, Sukarno's ties to Communist China had many people concerned.

In September 1965, an attempted military coup by the Communists escalated the worry of the Indonesians. The Communists kidnapped, tortured, and killed six generals and the young daughter of one of the generals. A general named Thojib Suharto took over as Indonesia's leader and forced Sukarno to resign in 1966. He was put under house arrest until his death in 1970. In response to the coup, the military coordinated with Islamic youth groups the mass murders of all Communist Party members and many ethnic Chinese throughout the entire archipelago. More than 1 million were imprisoned without trial if they had suspected Communist ties, and between 500,000 and 1 million were killed in 1965 and 1966.

A Time for Reform

For thirty-two years, Suharto ruled Indonesia. When Suharto was elected once again in 1998, the people objected violently. *"Reformasi!"* they cried. (Reform!) After going through an economic crisis the year before, they wanted new leadership. They had watched helplessly as factories closed and banks collapsed. Unemployment and food prices had soared. At Suharto's reelection, there were riots. In three days, 6,000 buildings were destroyed and hundreds of people died. On May 21, 1998, Suharto resigned. Vice President B. J. Habibie

Students protest Suharto's regime in 1998.

ruled for a short time, but he was replaced during the October 1999 election by Muslim leader Abdurrahman Wahid. Later, Suharto was formally charged with embezzling $570 million in state funds. Some believe he and his family stole close to $30 billion during his three decades of rule.

In 2001, Wahid was forced out of office for incompetence and financial scandals. Megawati Sukarnoputri, Sukarno's daughter, became ruler of the archipelago. She was the first woman president and had strong support from the youth sector. She coped with several important issues, including separatist movements and ongoing corruption. Most importantly, she worked out a relationship with Muslim political leaders who wanted Indonesia to become an Islamic state. Megawati wanted it to remain secular, with religious freedom for belief in God.

Indonesian president Megawati Sukarnoputri addressed the country's economy, corruption, and religious freedom during her presidency.

In October 2004, the country held its first direct presidential election, called a "modern day miracle" by a team from European Union's European Parliament. It was the nation's first peaceful and democratic election since 1955. More than 153 million registered voters turned out to vote. Megawati lost in a landslide to former army general and minister Susilo Bambang Yudhoyono. She accepted the defeat tearfully. Yudhoyono's top priorities are keeping the islands united and using the military to repress local independence movements, which he called "terrorist."

Searching for Unity

ALTHOUGH INDONESIA'S MOTTO IS *BHINNEKA TUNGGAL ikar*, or "unity through diversity," unity is one of its greatest challenges. How can a nation that is so split up geographically possibly be ruled? That question becomes even more complicated with the religious and ethnic differences found throughout the archipelago.

Opposite: **The Indonesian flag is raised during Independence Day celebrations in Jakarta.**

A Set of Principles

In 1945, Sukarno tried to rule through a set of principles and a unifying philosophy called Pancasila, or the Five Principles. He included it in most of his speeches and celebrations. The primary principle was Belief in One Supreme God. Indonesia offered freedom of worship for all faiths as long as they believed in a single god. Atheism was banned. Most Indonesians are Islamic; the rest are Christian, Hindu, or Buddhist. The second principle was Humanitarian Ideals. Neither individuals nor the nation itself could oppress or control any other human being, whether by physical force or through social or religious pressure. Third was National Unity. It asked the people of Indonesia to live together as one and to be loyal to

One of Sukarno's five principles is National Unity.

their entire nation. No group of any tribe, island, language, or skin color was superior to another. Fourth was Indonesian-Style Democracy, in which all Indonesians were encouraged to work together for common goals. They were to make governmental decisions by talking it over with each other until they reached a consensus. Last was Social Justice, which stated that Indonesia's natural resources were to be used for the benefit of everyone and that the weak should be protected by the strong. Although Pancasila was taught in every school and civil office, like many other admirable goals, it was too often ignored or distorted in practice.

The Coat of Arms

The Five Principles of Pancasila can be seen on Indonesia's coat of arms. The belief in one god is symbolized by a five-pointed gold star, while humanitarian ideals are seen in a gold chain made up of differently shaped links. The squares represent men; the circles represent women. National unity is found in the sacred banyan tree symbol, and Indonesian-style democracy is shown in the head of the *kanteng*, or wild bull. Social justice is symbolized by cotton and rice, the area's two main agricultural products.

The Structure of the Government

The Republic of Indonesia is a representative democracy with three branches of government. They have gone through some recent changes. The executive branch is headed by the president, who acts as both chief of state and head of the government. Until 2004, he was elected every five years by a legislative body called the People's Consultative Assembly. As Suharto's rules showed, there was no limit on how many times a person could be reelected. In 2004, however, the first presidential election in which candidates were chosen through the direct vote of citizens was held. Unlike in some countries, where presidential campaigns go on for almost a year, in Indonesia, campaigning is restricted to a mere three days. The voting age is seventeen.

The president of Indonesia appoints a cabinet of ministers who help to govern the country. If a national emergency arises, the president can issue orders that people must obey. The armed forces support the president.

The legislative branch is ruled by the People's Consultative Assembly. This group of people meets annually to review constitutional issues and every five years to look over general outlines of national policy. It contains 700 members, and 500 of them create the House of People's Representatives. The majority are chosen by voters, although 38 seats are

An Acehnese woman votes for president in the 2004 elections, the first election where Indonesians directly elected their new leader.

Great Indonesia

When Wage Rudolf Supratman composed the anthem *Indonesia Raya*, or "Great Indonesia," in 1928, it signified a cry for unity. At a time in their history when the islands were divided through language, ethnic, cultural, and religious differences, this song encouraged togetherness. It was sung at political rallies, and Indonesian youth latched onto it quickly as a sign of hope for the future.

Indonesia, my native land
My place of birth
Where I stand guard
Over my motherland

Indonesia, my nationality
My people and my country
Let us all cry
For united Indonesia

Long live my land
Long live my country
My nation and all my people

Arouse their spirit
Arouse their bodies
For Great Indonesia

Great Indonesia
Free and independent
The land, the country I love

Great Indonesia
Free and independent
Long live Indonesia

reserved for the military. The remaining 200 in the House are appointed. They are made up of provincial politicians and interest groups such as farmers, businessmen, and students.

The judicial branch has recently undergone some major changes. It is headed by the *Mahkamah Agung*, or Supreme Court. All justices are appointed by the president from a list of names approved by the legislature. In August

NATIONAL GOVERNMENT OF INDONESIA

Executive Branch

THE PRESIDENT

CABINET OF MINISTERS

Legislative Branch

PEOPLE'S CONSULTATIVE ASSEMBLY
(700 MEMBERS)

HOUSE OF PEOPLE'S REPRESENTATIVES
(500 MEMBERS)

Judicial Branch

SUPREME COURT

CONSTITUTIONAL COURT

Indonesia's Supreme Court oversees the country's judicial system. This photo shows Indonesia's Constitutional Court.

2003, a separate Constitutional Court was set up. In March 2004, the Supreme Court took responsibility for the financial and administrational duties of the lower court system, previously handled by the Ministry of Justice and Human Rights.

Below the Supreme Court are fourteen appeals courts, and under them are multiple district courts. Although criminal cases are tried in court under traditional law, civil cases are settled under *adat* law, an unwritten set of rules based on traditional local customs.

A Growing Number of Political Parties

When Indonesia became a nation in 1950, there were many political parties throughout Sukarno's presidency. The Government Party, Golkar, was most powerful. A second party represented Islamic organizations, and a third party, the Nationalists, was popular with youth and Christians. The largest party before 1965 was the Communist Party, with 20 million members. Only three parties were allowed to exist after 1967, when the Communist Party was banned. After 1998, the number of political parties rose dramatically. By 2004, more than forty parties were registered for the national election. There are still three broad groups that define themselves as government, Islamic, or nationalist.

The Face of the Newly Elected Ruler

The man who earned the title of president is a familiar one in Indonesia. Susilo Bambung Yudhoyono, or SBY as he is called, has been involved in the government for several decades. The son of an army officer, he graduated from the Indonesia Military Academy in 1973. Two years later, he was one of the men who helped invade East Timor. Although there were rumors of his involvement in possible war crimes during that attack, they were never proven.

In the 1980s, SBY went to the United States and received his master's degree in business management at Webster University in Missouri. He returned to his homeland and, between 1995 and 2000, held a number of important government positions including Chief Military Observer in Bosnia, Chief of Armed Forces Social and Political Affairs Staff, Minister of Mines, and, under Wahid, Minister for Security and Political Affairs. He was sometimes called the "thinking general."

In 2001, Wahid, under threat of impeachment, asked SBY to declare a state of emergency. SBY refused and was subsequently fired. When Megawati came to

power, she rehired him as Senior Political and Security Minister. He was put in charge of tracking down and arresting the people involved in the 2002 bombing in Bali. The dedication he gave to finding the criminals and the passionate speech he delivered at the attack's one-year anniversary impressed many people. When he resigned from his position in March 2004 after a public argument with Megawati and her husband, he enhanced his reputation for being a man of principle. In 2004, he won the election by a landslide. He chose Jusef Kalla for his vice president.

The Drive for Further Independence

When Indonesia declared its independence in 1945, the island of Timor was a complicated area. The western half officially belonged to Indonesia, but the eastern half was controlled by Portugal. When Portugal finally left the area thirty years later, Indonesia moved in immediately and attacked East Timor's capital of Dili. In December 1975, the military moved in, and by summer of the following year, it declared East Timor as its own province. It was a hard-won victory. As many as 200,000 Timorese people died from battle, starvation, or disease.

For many years, Timor belonged to Indonesia, although some refused to accept it. Everything changed when Suharto was replaced with President Habibie. Against the stringent advice of his military, he arranged it so that Indonesia and Portugal signed an agreement in 1999 allowing the people of East Timor to speak out. They could either vote for greater self-government as part of Indonesia or for complete independence

The Man Who Unified Indonesia

Sukarno (1901–1970), the man who would eventually become the first president of the Republic of Indonesia, was born in Surabaya. During high school, he met many of the era's nationalist leaders. After he graduated, instead of following his classmates to further education in the Netherlands, he studied engineering and architecture at the Bandung Technical College. There, he wrote articles urging unity in Indonesia in order to obtain independence.

In 1927, Sukarno helped establish the Indonesian Nationalist Party. By the end of the year, that organization was the main voice of nationalism. When Sukarno was arrested and convicted for disturbing the peace in 1929, his defense speech became considered to be a classic.

Sukarno returned to Jakarta in 1942, and thanks to radio access, he soon became well known throughout Indonesia as a leader and the creator of the Pancasila philosophy. By 1945, Indonesians believed he was the only person who could unify the islands and serve as president.

On August 17, 1945, Sukarno announced Indonesia's independence, but that was not the end of its troubles for five years. Multiple parties struggled for power, and finally Sukarno declared martial law. Fighting continued for years, and thousands of people were either killed or imprisoned. On March 11, 1966, Sukarno reluctantly signed a document guaranteed to end the riots and to pass the presidency over to General Suharto. He left with a badly tarnished reputation and died four years later.

Timorese cheer as UN troops arrive to help bring order to Timor after Indonesian military invasions.

from the country. Almost 80 percent voted for independence.

Their victory was short-lived. Outraged, Indonesian military invaded and proceeded to destroy everything, including the capital city. Buildings were burned, businesses were ransacked, and people fled in terror. More than 100,000 East Timorese were either killed or simply disappeared from the area. Many were taken as prisoners of war. Although the United Nations sent troops to restore order, the damage was done. East Timor and its people were shattered.

In 2002, the first presidential elections were held in East Timor. Jose Alexandre "Xanana" Gusmao won, and in May, that half of the island became an independent nation. Foreign peacekeepers are still there to help reclaim their country.

Timor is not the only island to strive for independence from Indonesia. Irian Jaya, now known as West Papua, and Aceh have also fought similar battles, but with less success.

West Papua is on the western half of New Guinea, the world's largest tropical island. It did not become a part of Indonesia when they proclaimed independence in 1945. Instead, it remained under Dutch control for another eighteen years. In 1961, it briefly declared its independence, but Indonesia took control two years later. During the 1970s and 1980s, many Papuans objected to being part of the country and formed the Free Papua Movement. They continued to try and separate, and in the process, thousands were killed. During 1999 and 2000, more died or were injured. When pro-independence leader Theys Eluay was murdered in 2001, there was rioting. As recently as December 2004, members of the Free

Iranese protest in Jakarta for a free Papua.

Papua Movement raised their flag of independence at a national celebration and refused to take it down even when ordered by the police.

On the northern corner of Sumatra is Aceh. It, too, wants independence from Indonesia. The people feel that Indonesia's central government has exploited their natural resources of oil and gas without any benefit to them. Although the nation has offered Aceh greater autonomy, or self-government, that is not enough. The fight of the Free Aceh Movement continues today but has made little progress.

The National Flag

The national flag of Indonesia is called the *Sang Saka Merah Putih*, which means "lofty bicolor of red and white." It has two equal horizontal bands with red on the top and white on the bottom. The red represents courage, freedom, and human blood. The white stands for purity, justice, and the human spirit. It was based on the flag used in the Javan Majapahit Empire, which had nine red and white stripes. This flag was officially adopted on September 17, 1945.

Jakarta: Did You Know This?

Jakarta, situated on Java, is Indonesia's capital and largest city, as well as its economic and cultural center. It is truly a mixture of the old and the new. It began in the 1300s as a small harbor under Hindu rule, called Sunda Kelapa. By the 1500s, it had turned into a major seaport and had been renamed Jayakarta, or "Glorious Victory" by its Muslim conquerors.

In 1618, most of Jakarta was destroyed by the Dutch, who built the new city of Batavia in its place. Batavia served as the center of the Dutch colonial empire for more than 300 years. The city's name was changed to its present name of Jakarta during the Japanese occupation of the 1940s.

Today, a little over half of the city's population lives in neighborhoods called *kampungs*. These resemble villages and are usually inhabited by people of the same ethnic group. Some kampungs are overcrowded slums whose bamboo shacks lack running water and electricity. Others are middle-class communities with stone houses and tiled roofs. The center of the city is jammed with high-rise buildings of glass and steel. There are

modern shopping centers (below), as well as old-fashioned markets where people can buy fish, anchors, ropes, and sea shells. Thirteen rivers flow through the city, and broad highways cut through the downtown. Traffic jams are a familiar sight. The people who live there often refer to their city as the "big durian," after

the foul-smelling Asian fruit with spiky skin and a sour taste. As awful as it may seem, they love the fruit—as they love their city.

Jakarta's main tourist attractions include the Monas, or National Monument, the National Museum of Indonesia, and the Ragunan Zoo.

Population (2004 est.): 12,296,000
Average Daily Temperature: 75°F (24°C)
Average Annual Rainfall: 71 inches (180 cm)

Java Sea

Jakarta Bay

Pelni Passenger Terminal

MARUNDA

ANCOL

Fine Arts Museum

ROROTAN

GLODOK

JELAMBAR

GROGOL

Stadium

Jakarta Fairgrounds

KEMAYORAN

SUNTER

SENEN

KELAPA GADING

CAKUNG

TOMANG

Monas (National Monument)

National Museum

US Embassy

MENTENG

PULO MAS

PULO GADUNG

PULO GEBANG

SLIPI

RAWAMANGUN

SENAYAN

KARET

MANGGARAL

JATINEGARA

KLENDER

KEBAYORAN BARU

KUNINGAN

TEBET

DUREN SAWIT

PONDOK KELAPA

KEMANG

CAWANG

HIALIM

CAWANG

PONDOK INDAH

SOS Medika Klinik

CILILITAN

Halim Perdana Kusuma International Airport

PONDOK GEDE

CILANDAK

CONDET

LEBAK BULUS

PONDOK LABU

Ragunan Zoo

CIRACAS

CIPAYUNG

0   2 miles

0   2 kilometers

Jakarta

CHAPTER SIX

A Slow but Steady Recovery

70

INDONESIA IS ONE OF THE RICHEST COUNTRIES IN THE WORLD when it comes to natural resources. It has fertile soils and abundant rainfall, as well as extensive forests full of teak, sandalwood, and ebony; waters swarming with fish; and vast reserves of oil, natural gas, rubber, and minerals. For the last four decades, there has been a growing shift away from agriculture as industrial development expands. Although 40 percent of Indonesians still work in some form of agriculture, employment in the civil services is growing. The county has had to deal with severe inflation due to a monetary crisis that swept through Asia in 1997 and 1998. Today, recovery is on the horizon, but more than one out of four Indonesians still lives in poverty. Unemployment runs over 10 percent and yet, each year, another 1.7 million youth enter the economy looking for jobs.

Until 1997, Indonesia was on a steady economic path with an annual growth of 7 to 8 percent. Everything changed when the financial disaster hit Asia. Bank systems collapsed, foreign debt soared, and bankruptcies flourished. Unemployment rose to a frightening 23 percent, and inflation reached 80 percent. There was large-scale poverty throughout Indonesia. Over 100 million people lived below the poverty level, defined as not having enough money to be able to buy food. Investors fled, as did tourists. To complicate matters, Suharto was accused of using government funds for his own use.

Opposite: **Almost half of all Indonesians work in agriculture. These workers are harvesting rice, the country's leading crop.**

Out with the Old, In with the New

In 1999, Indonesia began changing its banknotes one by one. Although the face of Suharto is gone, the bright colors remain. Most of the notes have images of historically important Indonesians on one side, with scenes of monuments and landscapes on the back. The 100-rupiah banknote has a burnt orange ship at sail on the front, with an image of Krakatoa on the back. The 1000 rupiah banknote offers a beautiful sailing image on the back and the 50,000 rupiah (right) a portrait of Wage Rudolf Supratman, composer of Indonesia's national anthem.

Denominations range from the 100 rupiah banknote—the most commonly used currency—and 500,

1000, 5000, 10,000, 20,000, 50,000 and 100,000 banknotes. Coins are considered to be inefficient, and the system depends entirely on banknotes.

As of January 7, 2005, 9,677 rupiah were equal to U.S.$1.

Recovery has been slow. In 1999, Indonesia reported no growth, but by 2000, the economy was up to 4 percent. Unemployment hovers around 10 percent, and inflation has gradually reduced to 6.6 percent.

Farming, Fishing, and Forestry

Not long ago, almost all Indonesians were involved in some aspect of agriculture. For the last forty years, this has been changing. Now, less than half hold jobs related to farming.

Indonesia's biggest crop is rice, which is grown in two different ways. The upland peoples of the outer islands practice dry rice farming, or "slash and burn." This type has existed for centuries. With this method, farmers cut the forest vegetation, let it dry, and then burn it. New crops are planted in the ashes. Most pieces of land can be used for two or three years using

Weights and Measures

Indonesia uses the metric system.

this technique, and then the soil must be left alone until it can build up nutrients again. On the inner islands, farmers use wet-rice cultivation. There is no burning involved; instead, an irrigation system is created. Since the soil is not stripped of its nutrients, several crops are produced each year. Men and women work together on the farms. While men do the plowing, women

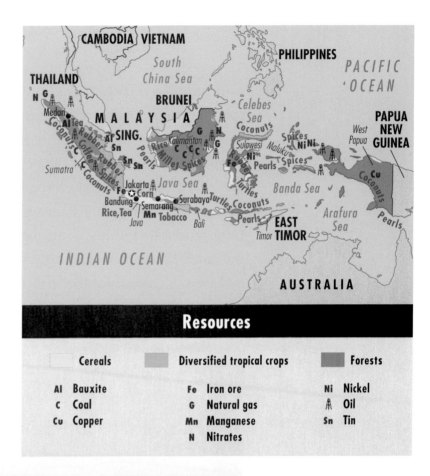

One way of growing rice is by wet-rice cultivation.

plant and weed. Before mechanical harvesting was invented, they also picked the rice by hand.

Other crops are grown in Indonesia, including cassava, corn, sage, soybeans, and sweet potatoes. Horses, pigs, chickens, and cattle are raised on the Lesser Sunda Islands. Poultry, beef, pork, and eggs are some of the country's biggest agricultural products. Fishing continues to be a large market, from the small-scale individual fishermen to the large-scale corporate export companies that process thousands of fish daily.

These fishermen will sell their catch at a local village.

Agriculture

Rice	51,000,000 metric tons
Cassava	16,347,000 metric tons
Corn	9,169,000 metric tons

Manufacturing

Cement	22,789,000 metric tons
Fertilizer	11,464,000 metric tons
Paper and plywood	6,978,000 metric tons

Mining

Natural gas	70,600 cubic meters
Coal	70,700,000 metric tons
Oil	553 metric barrels

When the Dutch had control of the islands, some of the biggest exports were coffee, tea, sugar, and tobacco, and that is still the case. In addition, Indonesia is one of the world's major suppliers of rubber.

Mining, Manufacturing, and Tourism

Indonesia, the only Asian member of the Organization of Petroleum Exporting Countries (OPEC), provides almost 2 percent of the world's oil demands. Crude oil and natural gas bring in the greatest amount of money, and almost all of it is found in Sumatra. Production is handled by the state-owned company Pertamina. In recent years, the government has

As the only Asian member of OPEC, Indonesia contributes 2 percent of the world's oil.

been trying to reduce its dependence on income from oil and has invited foreign investors to build factories and to hire young Indonesian men and women.

The soil of Indonesia is rich with some of the world's most sought-after minerals. Sumatra has coal and bauxite, the ore used to produce aluminum. Sulawesi has nickel; copper is found in West Papua. Tin, silver, zinc, and uranium are all also found there.

A lot of people head for the islands of Indonesia when it's time for vacation. The glittering water, the sandy beaches, and the lively culture all call out to be visited. The number of tourists is on the rise. In 2003, over $5.4 billion in foreign currency was spent on seeing Indonesian wonders.

Of all the islands in the archipelago, Bali draws the most visitors. Java and Sumatra are also popular destinations. While some come for sun and fun at the beach, others come to see the magnificent monuments and historical sites or to enjoy surfing, white-water rafting, or other water sports.

Tourists ride through the rain forest on Sumatra

The Buddhist Monastery on the Hill

Twenty-five miles (40 km) northwest of Yogykarta in central Java lies Indonesia's most popular tourist attraction. Borobudur, from the Sanskrit *Vihara Buddha Uhr*, or Buddhist Monastery on the Hill, is a Buddhist relic that amazes and enthralls the hundreds of people who go to see it.

Borobudur is almost 1,200 years old. Built between A.D. 750 and 850, it has survived everything from earthquakes to angry terrorists to curious tourists. The building sits on a base 387 feet (118 m) by 387 feet and rises up ten levels. It took hundreds of thousands of men to complete it. Historians believe that more than 30,000 stonecutters and sculptors helped to create Borobudur, plus 15,000 men to carry 1.3 million blocks of stones and thousands of masons to position them.

Soon after the monument was finished, it was mysteriously abandoned. For centuries it was forgotten and covered under the ash from the eruption of Gunung Merapi. In 1815, Governor Raffles heard rumors of the site and spent two months removing dirt and vegetation in hopes of finding it. When he finally did, he was struck by its size and age and stopped the excavation because he was worried about damaging it. Once again Borobudur sat quietly until the Dutch attempted to restore it between 1907 and 1911. The monument's foundation was being eroded by rainfall and minerals, and finally the Dutch gave up too.

Borobudur's moment came in 1973, when UNESCO helped to sponsor a real excavation. It took $25 million and 700 men working six days a week for ten years to get the job done. Each one of the 1.3 million stones was removed, listed, photographed, cleaned, treated, and returned. A new foundation was built for support, and a drainage system was put in to prevent any further water damage.

In 1985, Suharto's enemies planted a number of bombs on the upper level of Borobudur. Although they exploded, the damage was minimal and has since been repaired completely. Today, visitors can walk through its terraced levels and admire the 504 images of Buddha found there. They slow down to appreciate the 1,460 intricately carved panels that tell the history of the land and the 1,212 that describe the philosophy of Buddhism.

From Here to There and Back Again

For countless years, people have traveled from one island to another in Indonesia. In the beginning, it was by ships on ancient trade routes. Today, for those who still want to use water to travel, the national company of Pelni offers ships that set sail on a daily, weekly, and monthly basis. For quick trips, many Indonesians use canoes. For others who prefer to fly, they can use the national airline, Garuda, named for a mythical bird. Indonesia has 661 airports and 22 heliports.

The island of Java has an excellent railroad system, thanks to the Dutch. It links all of the island's cities. Sumatra has railroads that run north and south. Because very few of the other islands have a railroad, many people depend on buses instead. The buses run regular routes with set stops, but if they happen to spot someone on the road that needs a ride, they will stop. Less than 1 percent of the entire population owns any kind of automobile. Although Indonesia has 212,950 miles (342,700 km) of highway, the best roads are found on Java, Bali, and Lombock. The roads on some of the other islands are often extraordinarily twisty and marred by potholes or landslides.

Many Indonesians depend on bicycles, motorcycles, or horse-drawn carts for transportation. Some used to hire *becaks*, or three-wheeled rickshaws pedaled by a driver sitting in the

Passengers in Jakarta rely on the railway system to connect them from city to city.

rear. In the 1980s, however, they were banned in places like Jakarta because of the confusion they caused in traffic. Rickshaws still exist in the smaller towns, and riders prefer them because they are quiet and pollution-free. In other cities, people ride on a *bajaj*, a

Becaks have been banned in some Indonesian cities, but they can still be found in some smaller towns.

motorized rickshaw. The engines in these are much like the engine of a lawnmower—and just as loud.

Keeping in Touch

In Indonesia, the government owns the postal, telegraph, and telephone systems. As of 2002, there were 7.75 million telephone lines and 11.7 million cell phones.

There are 41 broadcast television stations and 13.75 million television sets in Indonesia. Most sets are found in the cities, although villages sometimes may have a television set that everyone can watch. There is twice the number of radios as televisions in the archipelago (31.5 million). The national radio broadcasts 24 hours a day.

Indonesians have a variety of publications to choose from to read about current events.

Almost seventy daily newspapers are published throughout Indonesia. All are written in Bahasa Indonesian except for the *Jakarta Post* and the *Indonesian Observer*, which are written in English.

The Internet is slowly growing in this country. As of 2000, there were twenty-four Internet service providers and 8 million Indonesians online.

A World of Differences

EVEN THOUGH A PORTION OF INDONESIA IS MADE UP OF islands almost too little to see, it still manages to fit an estimated 238,452,952 people on it. It is the fourth most populated nation in the world, surpassed only by China, India, and the United States.

Most countries have a limited number of ethnic groups because they are all so closely located. They have a common language, culture, and history. The people of Indonesia, however, are separated by towering mountain ranges and countless miles of water. Because of this, Indonesia's ethnic groups number over an astounding 300. Within those groups, there are almost 400 languages. There are extraordinary differences

Opposite: **Indonesia is a country made up of many ethnic groups contributing to the culture and flavor of each island.**

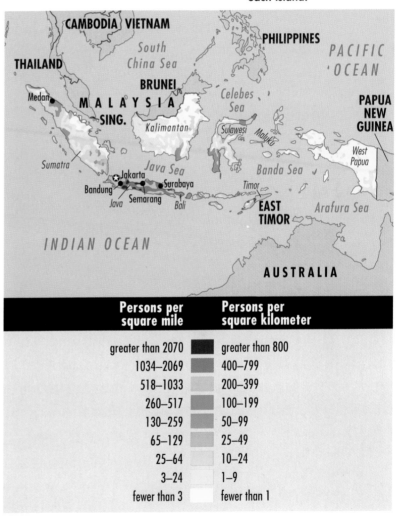

Persons per square mile		Persons per square kilometer
greater than 2070		greater than 800
1034–2069		400–799
518–1033		200–399
260–517		100–199
130–259		50–99
65–129		25–49
25–64		10–24
3–24		1–9
fewer than 3		fewer than 1

from one island to another, yet somehow, the people find a way to be united.

The People of the Archipelago

The largest ethnic group within Indonesia is the Javanese. They live in Central and Eastern Java and make up almost half of the country's entire population. Their numbers help them to dominate all of Indonesia's politics and military. Many military leaders and government officials have been Javanese, including all but one of their presidents.

Most Javanese earn their living through farming or factory work. They live in small villages of 300 or fewer. Because Java has always had a large population, it is rich in culture, art, and language. Etiquette is very important to them, and very young children are expected to learn proper respect for their elders or risk being disciplined. Speaking is almost an art for the Javanese, as they have three different levels of speech (formal,

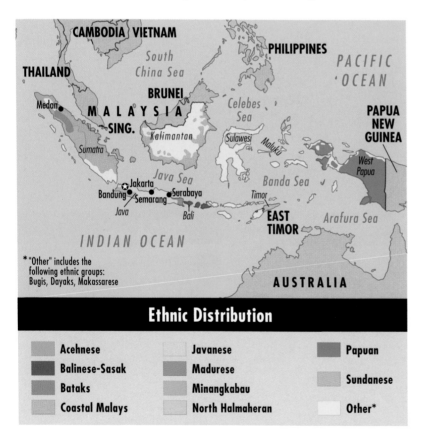

Ethnic Distribution

- Acehnese
- Balinese-Sasak
- Bataks
- Coastal Malays
- Javanese
- Madurese
- Minangkabau
- North Halmaheran
- Papuan
- Sundanese
- Other*

*"Other" includes the following ethnic groups: Bugis, Dayaks, Makassarese

semiformal, and informal), reflecting a person's rank, status, age, and the degree of familiarity between the two people.

The Javanese have a society largely based on rank. The aristocrats, or highest class, are called the *priyayi* or the *wong gedhe*, which means "important men." The island's peasants are called the *wong cilik*, or "little men," and in between the two are the *wong sodagar*, or merchants. Most Javanese are Muslims, although there are strong Catholic and Christian minorites.

Also located in the highlands of western Java are the Sudanese. They are the second largest ethnic group. They are a gentle people with a strong belief in magic, sorcery, and angry spirits. Because of their geographical nearness, the Sudanese are quite similar to the Javanese in ceremony, art, and music. They also have three levels of language, which are considered refined (*lemes*), medium (*sedang*), and vulgar (*kasar*).

Over in the isolated areas of Java are the Badui. These people are unique in their beliefs about the world. The villages at the center of the region are homes to those who think they are directly descended from gods. They want little to do with the outside world and spend most of their time with "slash and burn" farming. The outer villages have slightly more contact with other parts of Indonesia, but it is limited. None of the Badui has learned how to write, fearing that it somehow

The Javanese are Indonesia's largest ethnic group. Most are farmers or work in factories.

Bataks sing in a village near Lake Toba.

imparts a kind of magic power that is in conflict with their religious system of gods and spirits.

The island of Sumatra is home to four ethnic groups. The Achenese in the northernmost region are more rural than some. Their villages are often located in the middle of rice fields, and not surprisingly, many people are farmers. Others are weavers, potters, and boat builders. Here Islam runs right alongside a belief in magic and dreams. The Achenese have been fiercely independent throughout history and have fought brutal military occupation for over two decades.

Other groups on Sumatra include the Batak, the Minangkabau, and the Malays. The Batak live in the north-central region, and a number are Christian. Their homes are unusual—with trapdoors built into the floor and carved buffalo horns on the exterior. The Batak are emotional and dramatic people, so it is little surprise that many entertainers come from this area. In the highlands of west-central Sumatra are the Minangkabau. In this culture, the women rule; property, money, family names, and titles are passed down from mother

to daughter. Instead of a groom paying a price for a bride, the opposite is true, and after marriage, it is the man who goes to live with his wife's family. Mothers are greatly honored, and they believe that "Heaven is below the sole of the mother's foot," or, treat your mother badly and you won't go to heaven. Divorce and remarriage are commonplace in this society. The Malays live in bamboo huts atop wooden platforms that float up and down the rivers for trading and fishing.

Ethnic Breakdown in National Population

Javanese	47%
Sudanese	14%
Madurese	8%
Malays	8%
Minangkabau	3.3%
Bugis	2.6%
Balinese	2%
Batak	2%
Makassarese	1.1%
Dayaks	1%
Other minorities	11%

Population of Major Cities (2004)	
Jakarta in Java	12,296,000
Bandung in Java	3,409,000
Surabaya in Java	2,461,000
Medan in Sumatra	2,204,300
Semarang in Java	1,267,100

The Balinese of Bali are primarily Hindu. The majority are commoners, or *wong liya*. The others are part of a caste system. They have distinct villages dedicated to a kind of craft. For example, Ubud is home to painters, while Mas is the village of carvers. Their religion is *agama tirta*, or the religion of water.

Water is blessed by a priest for use in various ceremonies, and holy water is sprinkled during festivals. Trouble comes from spirits, and solutions come from magic. Death is celebrated with cremation and extravagant rituals. The Balinese live in a hereditary caste system; their class is determined by birth. The highest class is the *Brahmans*, high priests. The next class is the *Satriya*, descendants of warriors and rulers. The *Wesia* are merchants, and the *Sudra* are commoners. Sudra make up 90 percent of the Balinese population.

On the island of Sulawesi are the groups Buginese, Minahasa, and Torajanese. The Buginese are off the north and east coasts, and they have a rich history of pirating, trading, and colonizing. Many are still excellent seamen, able to sail by the power of the wind only and without a compass to direct them. They claim they can somehow smell when land is close. They also produce high-quality silk that is in high demand with natives and tourists alike. The northern part of Sulawesi is home to the Minahasa, an agricultural people. Although most are Christian, they still believe in the god of earth and the sun god. The Torajanese in central Sulawesi are like the old-fashioned mountain men, spending their time hunting and carving. The sign of the buffalo is their symbol, and they

A high Brahman priest prays inside a temple in Bali

wear headdresses of buffalo horns and give a buffalo to the groom in return for a bride. Funerals are important events in their culture, and their dead are usually placed up high in limestone cliffs to safeguard them.

Dayak is the name given to the 200 tribes living along Kalimantan. Unlike many of the other ethnic groups, they are non-Muslim and believe in ancestral spirits and animism. Shamans take care of their physical and mental illnesses, and rocks, water, and plants are thought to contain helpful spirits. Most Dayaks live in communal longhouses and make their living by hunting, fishing, and gathering forest produce. They capture animals through the ancient arts of spear and blowpipe. Historians consider them to be the original people of the jungle in this part of the world. Body decoration is important to them; they wear beads as well as tattoos. Many wear heavy metal earrings to make their earlobes dangle all the way to

Dayak women often have tattoos and wear heavy earrings that pull their earlobes below their shoulders.

their shoulders in order to look more attractive. They have very simple technology. Their tools and weapons are made of bamboo, stone, and iron.

On western Papua, the Irianese tribes live quite simply. They were discovered only sixty years ago, during World War II. Thousands of Allied troops, primarily Americans, came to the island to set up a military base and came across this quiet tribe. Three-quarters of the island is still covered in some of the densest forests in the world. Although the world had found the Irianese, they still cling to some ancient traditions, including wearing pigs' tusks in their noses and decorating their bodies with war paint.

Tribesmen on Irian Jaya wear war paint and live clinging to ancient traditions.

One Situation, Many Reactions

The *suku*, or ethnic groups, of Indonesia have different ways of reacting to the same situation. This anecdote shows their vast differences.

"A man had his toe trop upon. If he were Batak, he would scowl savagely and immediately vent his displeasure in loud, direct, abusive terms . . . and do nothing; if Javanese, he would clear his throat politely, gesture vaguely in the direction of the offended digit, call a large group around him, and arrive at a decision by consensus to possibly do something about it sometime; if he were Balinese, he would pray; if he were Bugis or Madurese, he would immediately beat up the person; if he were Padang, he would offer some money to make it right."

The Chinese Indonesians

Three percent of Indonesia's population is Chinese Indonesian. Their history has been a violent one. Although their numbers are small, they control almost 80 percent of the economy and are the wealthiest of the ethnic groups. Under Dutch rule, they were not allowed to own land and so focused on developing businesses. Today they operate shops, hotels, banks, and restaurants. Despite this success, the Chinese Indonesians have been the target of much violence throughout the years. During his reign, Suharto banned the Chinese language and stopped the Chinese press from publishing. Chinese names were changed to Indonesian, and Chinese schools were closed. Even Chinese festivals and customs were not allowed to be practiced in public, and the government refused to recognize Confucianism, one of the Chinese Indonesians' primary religions.

After Suharto's fall in 1999, some bans were lifted. Although Chinese New Year is now celebrated publicly, Chinese schools are still not allowed. In addition, the Chinese

Indonesians have been attacked in several riots. In 1965, they were suspected of being Communists and were attacked. In 1998, they were criticized for being successful businesspeople and were viciously attacked as their businesses were destroyed. Many fled the islands, but returned later to be with family and to start over again.

An Indonesian woman of Chinese descent prays at a temple.

The Language of Bahasa Indonesia

In 1928, Bahasa Indonesia was suggested as the country's national language by the emerging nationalist leaders in the hopes of bringing the people together. Seventeen years later, it became the country's official language. There are twelve major languages spoken throughout the archipelago: Javanese, Sudanese, Buginese, Makassarese, Balinese, Minahasen, and Ambonese. How a person speaks is often the main way to tell what ethnic group he or she belongs to. Despite the different languages, Bahasa Indonesia is the one the majority speak, and it gives the people a common way to communicate.

Bahasa Indonesia is a simple language compared with many. There are no genders, words sound as they are spelled, and are written in the Roman alphabet. Because so many traders passed through the coasts of this archipelago, a number

From One Island to Another

A century ago, while Indonesia was still under Dutch control, more than 650,000 Javanese were forced to move to Sumatra in an attempt to solve the problem of overpopulation. Java had too many people, so why not move them to an island that had far fewer? That process is called transmigration. Although it shifted the population for a period of time, it was not welcomed. People did not want to be uprooted from their homes, family, and culture and forced to live elsewhere.

Overpopulation continued to plague the islands over the next hundred years. In 1963 and 1976, when Irian Jaya and East Timor were united with Indonesia, many Javanese were sent to those new provinces to live. The migrants were seen as unwelcome aliens, and ethnic conflicts were common as traditions, religion, and languages clashed. Between 1984 and 1989, 3.2 million Indonesians were resettled from Java and Bali to Sumatra, Kalimantan, and Sulawesi. Most of them were the country's poorest citizens, many homeless. Conflicts continued, and in 1997, the Madurese and the Dayaks of Kalimantan battled fiercely. Hundreds were killed.

The problem of too many people and not enough room is an ongoing issue in Indonesia. Over half of all the people live on Java, and more than 2,500 people are squeezed into every square mile. Although transmigration is no longer forced, the government encourages families to move by offering them a home and 5 acres (2 ha) of land at their new location.

The problem is further complicated by Indonesia's birthrate. At the time of its independence, the population growth rate was 3 percent, meaning that it could double every twenty-five years. In the 1960s, a family planning campaign was launched to show the people the wisdom of limiting how many children they had. The motto "Two is enough" was put on posters and on the 5-rupiah coin.

By the 1990s, the population growth rate began to fall. It is currently 1.5 percent. The decline is said to be due to a combination of the family planning messages and increased use of birth control, as well as women's staying in school for longer periods and putting off motherhood.

of words from other cultures have made their way into the vocabulary. Bahasa Indonesia is spoken in government, the media, in business, and in school. It is taught until the third grade, and then English becomes the primary language.

Although the Indonesian language is a fairly simple one, it is occasionally complicated by multiple ways to say one word. For example, there are many different ways to say hello. How Indonesians greet each other depends on the time of day. *Selamat pagi* means good morning; *selamat siang* means good afternoon; *selamat sore* means good evening, and *selamat malam* means good night.

Indonesians do not like to say no, so they have developed a dozen ways to avoid it. They will say *tidak* (a negative usually used with other words), *belum* (not yet), *tidak usah* (not necessary), *lebih baik tidak* (not a good idea), *tidak boleh* (not allowed to), *tidak senang* (not happy), *tidak terima* (don't approve), *jangan* (don't!), *bukan* (who did this?), *enggak* (no, a low Javanese word), *terima kasih* (no, thank you) and *maaf tidak* (no, sorry). They even have half a dozen ways to say please!

Common Words and Phrases

Namanya siapa?	What is your name?
Senagn ketemu.	Nice to meet you.
Dari mana?	Where are you from?
Agama anda apa?	What is your religion?
Berapa harganya?	How much does this cost?
Jam berapa sekarang?	What time is it?
Terima kasih.	Thank you.
Ma'af.	I'm sorry.
Sampai jumpa lagi.	Till we meet again.

The Roman alphabet is used to spell words in Bahasa Indonesia.

"Belief in One, Supreme God"

IN INDONESIA, RELIGION IS SUCH A PART OF LIFE THAT IT affects politics, culture, and the economy. In 1945, the new constitution that declared the country's independence stated that its people believed in "One, Supreme God." Twenty years later, Suharto announced that every single Indonesian must claim a religion. If they refused, they would be labeled either an atheist—a person who does not believe in any God—or a Communist and would be killed.

Almost all of the people of Indonesia follow one of four religions: Islam, Christianity (Protestantism and Roman Catholicism), Hinduism, and Buddhism. Atheism is banned, but animism, or the belief in nature spirits, can still be found on some of the most isolated islands, such as west Sumba and parts of Papua. Animists believe that powerful spirits live inside natural elements such as trees, rocks, rivers, the sun, and the rain. They also believe in the presence of ghosts, genies, goddesses, and demons.

Opposite: **A worshipper prays at a temple ceremony in Bali.**

The Religions of the Islands

Islam	88%
Protestantism	5%
Roman Catholicism	3%
Hinduism	2%
Buddhism	1%
Other religions	1%

The Pillars of Islam

The religion of Islam first arrived in Indonesia through the traders who came to the coasts of northern Sumatra. Slowly, it spread inland to the courts, and by the end of the fourteenth century it had reached the entire archipelago. Those who still believed in Hinduism and Buddhism were pushed into the more remote parts of Indonesia. Islam continued to grow, and by the time the country declared its independence, it was the primary religion. By the 1990s, Indonesia was the world's largest Islamic country.

An Act of Terrorism

The night of October 12, 2002, will live on in the memories of many countries around the world. At 11:05 P.M., an electronically triggered bomb worn in the jacket of an Islamic man exploded in the middle of Paddy's Bar in Kuta, a city in Bali. As people poured out of the bar, another bomb, inside a van in front of the Sari Club, exploded. More than 200 people were killed, and another 200 were injured. Most were vacationers, representing 22 different nationalities. When the numbers were added up, the dead included 38 Indonesians, 88 Australians, 7 Americans, and 23 English, as well as many from other countries.

In the months to come, blame was narrowed to an Islamic group associated with al Qaeda. Leader Abu Baker Bashir was called the Osama bin Laden of Southeast Asia. Soon other names followed. By the end of 2003, all of the accused had been through the courts. Several were put to death, while others were given life imprisonment.

The event was a tragic spot in Indonesian history that will be long remembered. It especially affected the livelihoods of many Balinese, as tourism dropped dramatically. It is something that President SBY keeps in mind as he addresses the issue of ongoing terrorism.

People who practice Islam are called Muslims. They are led by the word of the prophet Muhammad, who was not a god but a human chosen by God to spread His word through the Quran, or holy book. Muslims believe that Jesus, Noah, Abraham, David, and Solomon were also prophets.

Islam is based primarily on a system of moral principles. All Islamic law comes from the Quran. There are no requirements to be Muslim other than following its basic tenets. Indonesia practices a much more relaxed style of Islam than some other countries.

There are five duties, or pillars, of Islam. First, a Muslim must recite, "There is no god but God, and Muhammad is the messenger of God" every day. Second, they must pray five times a day: sunrise, noon, late afternoon, twilight, and nightfall. Loudspeakers throughout most cities announce a reminder, and it is also broadcast over the radio and television

The second pillar of Islam is to pray five times per day.

and printed in the newspapers. A man called a *muezzin* cries out a call to prayer; men head toward mosques, while women and children pray at home. All prayers are said in Arabic while facing in the direction of the holy city of Mecca in Saudi Arabia.

The third step of Islam is charity. Two and a half percent of a person's income is to be given to the poor each year. The fourth tenet is self-purification or fasting. Muslims are not to eat, drink, or smoke from dawn to dusk during the month of Ramadan. In addition to this, each Friday, a ritual is performed before prayer. The hands are washed first, followed by the mouth, face, arms up to the elbows, and feet up to the ankles. The head is wet and the hair is combed. If this process is interrupted or done out of order, a person must start all over again.

A Fight for Religion

Cockfighting is a sport where two roosters are put in a pit to fight to the death. Although it is officially illegal in Indonesia, as well as in many other parts of the world, people are still able to host a fight if it is done as part of a religious ceremony. It is often held at night outside a temple. People hope the sacrifice will satisfy the demons so they don't bother the community. These cocks are specially bred and trained for fighting. A razor or sharp metal spur is tied to one claw of each bird, and the fight does not end until one of the cocks is killed. Indonesians often bet large amounts of money on these cockfights, which is one of the main reasons the government has tried to outlaw the sport. Cockfighting is especially widespread in Bali. Men in Bali and some parts of Java consider it a favorite gambling sport.

The fifth step in Islam is that of *hajj*, or pilgrimage. Muslims must make a journey to Mecca at least once in their lifetime. Each year, hundreds of thousands make the long trip.

Hinduism and Buddhism

The island of Bali has more Hindus than any other place on earth besides India. Hindus do not separate their religion from the rest of their lives. It is a part of everything they do. Their beliefs are based less on law and scripture and more on art and

Brahma is the Hindu Creator god

ritual. They have multiple gods, including Brahma, the Creator; Vishnu, the Preserver; and Shiva, the Destroyer. They believe in reincarnation, or the ability to live many lifetimes, as well as the presence of ancestral spirits. Often their faith is expressed through *wayang*, or shadow puppets, that tell the story of their faith's history. They have elaborate ceremonies for each stage of their lives, from birth and puberty to marriage and death.

There are not many Buddhists left in Indonesia, even though it was the primary religion before Islam. Buddhism was founded in the sixth century by an Indian prince named Siddhartha Gautama, later known as Buddha. He felt that no temple or priest was needed to practice religion. Instead, people

The Beauty of the Hindu

Twenty minutes from Yogyakarta City in central Java is a group of Hindu temples that were built between the eighth and tenth centuries. They are known as the Prambanan Temple compounds. Locally, they are called the *Loro Jongrang*, or "Slender Virgin." Shortly after being built, these huge temples were abandoned and largely forgotten. Over the decades, they began to fall apart. An earthquake in the mid-sixteenth century only toppled them further. Treasure hunters and locals commonly helped themselves to whatever they wanted from the site.

Reconstruction of the site began in 1918 and continues today. There are three main temples, and they are dedicated to the Hindu gods of Shiva, Vishnu, and Brahma. The largest one, in the middle, is *Candi Siva Mahadeva*. It stands at 155 feet (47 m). On the north side is the *Candi Vishnu*, and on the south is *Candi Brahma*. All of them have intricate, detailed carvings that tell the story of the Hindu religion. This temple is on the UNESCO World Heritage List as of 1991.

simply had to follow the Four Noble Truths and the Eightfold Path and it would lead them to enlightenment, as it did for him. The Truths are that life is full of suffering, and suffering is due to the constant craving for worldly objects. Suffering ends when craving stops. Enlightenment comes when a person has reflected this knowledge through his resolve, speech, conduct, livelihood, effect on others, mindfulness, concentration, and perspectives. Today, most Buddhists in Indonesia are Chinese Indonesians.

Twofold Christianity

In Indonesia, Christians practice either Roman Catholicism or Protestantism, religions that were brought to the archipelago 400 years ago. When the Dutch defeated Portugal in 1605, Catholic missionaries were expelled from the country. It was not until the twentieth century that they returned to the islands.

During the changeover of power in 1965, all Indonesians were forced to choose a religion. If they did not, they would be considered communist sympathizers. Not sure what to do, some turned to Christian churches. Today, most of the Catholics are found on the island of Flores.

The Ceremony of Kasada

One of the most beautiful places in Indonesia is found in Tenegger, at the center of East Java. Two peaked volcanoes are there, one that erupted long ago, leaving a huge, cauldronlike empty space filled with gray sand, appropriately named the Sand Sea. The two peaks are the inactive Mount Batok and the active Mount Bromo.

Besides being a tourist attraction, Mount Bromo is the site of Kasada, the Tenggerese's annual holy ceremony. This small ethnic group practices a combination of Hinduism and Buddhism. Once a year, they gather at the base of Mount Bromo to present offerings of rice, fruit, and vegetables to the God of the Mountain, *Hyang Widi Wasa*. A classical ballet performance is held to recount their religious legends, and a new priest is chosen.

According to the legend, the ceremony of Kasada began during the time of the Majapahit Kingdom. The queen had a daughter named Roro Anteng, and when she grew up, she married a young man named Joko Seger and settled in East Java. Although they loved each other, they were unhappy because they had no children. They climbed to the top of Mount Borno and prayed to the God of the Mountain for help. The god assured them that they would have many children, but only on the condition that they would sacrifice the youngest one to him. The queen had twenty-five children and, under threat of disaster, gave Kesuma, the youngest, to the volcano. The child's voice was heard to say, "I have been sacrificed by our parents to appear before Hyang Widi. Be in peace and live prosperously, never forgetting to perform worship. As a reminder, I ask you to perform an annual ceremony on the fourteenth day of Kasada at the time of the half-moon bringing offering of crops and livestock."

CHAPTER NINE

A Culture of Celebration and Tradition

BECAUSE INDONESIA HAS SUCH A RICH BACKGROUND IN history, it has an even more amazing culture. Each island has its own traditions, but many types of celebration, rites of passage, and entertainment are shared among the islands.

Opposite: **Palace dancers, who perform for royalty, act out scenes from the Hindu epic *The Ramayana*.**

Novelist Pramoedya Ananta Toer was jailed during Suharto's reign for speaking out against his country's policies.

So It Is Written

Like with many early cultures, Indonesia's original literature consisted of folk tales and legends handed down by word of mouth. When Islam reached the archipelago, poems written in Malay came with it. As the pressure for independence grew, more citizens began to write to express their frustration and hope. Between 1942 and 1965, literature exploded with prolific writings about revolution. A group called *Lekra* was formed and led, in part, by novelist Pramoedya Ananta Toer. In 1965, Suharto banned the group and sent Toer to prison.

Another writer imprisoned for his words was Mochtar Lubis. He began writing when Indonesia was under Japanese control. He wrote everything from letters and newspaper articles to short stories and an autobiography. He was put in prison in 1956 and again in 1975 for his outspoken criticism of his country.

The Poet of "I Want to Live Another Thousand Years"

One of the most honored and respected writers in Indonesia is a man named Anwar Chairil (1922–1949). Born in East Sumatra, he began writing poems as a young child. His most famous one is "Aku," written in 1943. Although it was originally inspired by separation from his father, many Indonesians used it in their fight for freedom.

"Aku"

If my time should come
I'd like no one to entice me
Not even you
No need for those sobs and cries
I am but a wild animal
Cut from its kind
Though bullets should pierce my skin
I shall strike and march forth
Wounds and poison shall I take aflee. Aflee
'til the pain and pang should disappear
And I should care even less
I want to live
For another thousand years.

During his short lifetime, Chairil worked on the editorial board of the literary journal *Siasat* and was quite active in a variety of political and patriotic issues. Much of his poetry centered around those themes, as in "Dipo Negro": "Better destruction than slavery/Better extermination than oppression./The hour of death can be an hour of new birth:/To be alive, you have to taste living."

Gamelan musicians perform
in Bali

The Sound of Music

Music is an integral part of Indonesian culture. Different styles
can be heard from island to island, large city to small village.
Gamelan is known across the entire archipelago as the traditional Indonesian music. Legend states that it was first
invented by a Javanese king in the third century. A gamelan
orchestra is made up of five to eighty percussive instruments.
There are large bronze gongs either hung by ropes and struck
with mallets or lying flat in a wooden frame, along with xylo-
phones and many kinds of drums. Some orchestras feature a
female singer. Gamelan music is heard everywhere in mosques
and as accompaniment for ceremonies and important events.

Masked dancers tell the story of the great Hindu epic *The Ramayana*

Other types of music heard in Indonesia are *dangdut* and *jaipongan*. Dangdut is a combination of Malay, Western rock, Indian film scores, and Arab pop. The youth like it best, especially because the performers are often quite glamorous. Jaipongan is also popular with the younger people. It began in western Java in the 1970s and uses gongs, drums, and shouting.

Where there is music, there is often dance. Most dances are done to tell a story. Masked dances, where performers wear animal faces, are one of the country's oldest traditions. In central Java, performers dance while behaving like historical characters and singing in a poetic language that is sometimes referred to as Javanese opera.

Some Indonesian tribes perform ritual dancing for special events. Priests and priestesses may lead a dance to celebrate a birth or wedding, as well as to mourn a death. Harvesttime is cause for dance, as is preparing for battle or exorcising a demon.

Ladies perform a dance at a funeral ceremony.

A Culture of Celebration and Tradition **107**

The Art and Style of Didik Nini Thowok

When it comes to entertaining people, Didik Nini Thowok knows just what to do. As a dancer, choreographer, comedian, mime, and television star, he keeps his audience smiling. Known as one of Indonesia's most famous entertainers, Thowok has performed in countries all over the world. Combining classical, folk, and modern dance with a good dose of comedy, he hopes to "cheer up the heart and the souls of the public." Currently, he is the director of the Vocational Dance Education of Natya Lakshia Institute, the Didik Nini Thowok Foundation, and Didik Nini Thowok Entertainment. He works to preserve the cultural heritage of his homeland through his skillful and diverse performances.

A nineteenth-century wayang shadow puppet

The World of Wayang

Many Indonesians believe that they reach the highest levels of spiritual achievement through art. This is especially true when it comes to wayang, or the art of puppetry. Performances always contain historical and sacred elements and are the country's primary form of entertainment.

There are a number of different kinds of puppetry performances, from *wayang kulit*, or shadow puppetry, performed behind a white cotton screen, to *wayang perjuangan*, which focuses on stories about the fight for independence. Wayang puppets are a work of art. Made out of buffalo hide pierced with multiple holes, they are painted with great detail in bright colors. They are flat and have sticks attached to their arms, legs, heads, and torsos in order to move. Each one has a very distinct personality.

The *dalang* is the talented storyteller and director who runs the entire show. Often he

A Beautiful Weapon

One of the most unusual weapons found in Indonesia is the *keris*. A cross between a sword and a dagger, it has a wavy blade and a jewel-encrusted handle. In the past, a keris was believed to have magical powers that were capable of protecting its owner from evil influences or possible danger. The more times it drew blood, the more powerful it was supposed to become. Balinese and Javanese aristocrats used to carry a keris to show their high rank. Today, the weapon is only carried in ceremonies. The owner of a keris takes great pride in ownership and will carefully clean it each time it is worn before returning it to its silk wrappings.

is operating more than forty puppets, plus singing and acting in performances that commonly run from dusk until dawn. It is little surprise that he charges high prices for his work.

A Reflection of Beauty

Where once Indonesia's art was a direct reflection of religion, today it is more of an expression of beauty—and a chance to make money. The country specializes in weaving. The fabrics found here are some of the world's most exquisite. Most are made out of cotton, and colors come from plants or minerals found in the region. Each cloth is unique in its design and pattern.

A woman uses the ikat method of weaving

Indonesia is renowned for its batik fabrics. Expert Indonesians also create beautiful cloth through the practice of *ikat* and *songket*. Ikat, which means knotting or binding, is made with threads that have been tie-dyed before they were used. The women who use this method need great skill and patience, as it is a slow, complex project. In some areas, these special threads can only be put on the loom on specific days, like those with a full moon or at highest tide, or else they may break and bring bad luck. Songket is a process of decorating fabric with a delicate pattern of gold and silver threads. Bali and Palembang are known internationally for their songket.

The Art of Dyeing

The most common form of textile production in Indonesia is batik. To make a unique piece of batik cloth, women first take a piece of plain cotton or silk and paint a design on it with wax (left). Next, they dip the cloth into dye, which colors the non-waxed portion of the fabric. The wax is then scraped off, and more wax is applied in a new design to a different section. Once again it is dipped in dye, although another color. This process of waxing, scraping, and rewaxing continues as long as the artist wants. There are more than 1,000 traditional designs of flowers, leaves, animals, diamonds, stars, and symbols.

Indonesians use batik for much of their clothing, as well as for everyday fabrics like tablecloths or wall hangings. A newly married couple is commonly wrapped together in a piece of batik to symbolize their unity.

A Culture of Celebration and Tradition **111**

A Balinese wood carver

Many Indonesians are wood craftsmen. Because the country has such rich timberland, they have a number of different types of wood to work with. They carve and sculpt shields, spirit poles, statues, and ceremonial beds. Others use stone and metal to create beautiful statues of their gods.

Women specialize in pottery and basketry. In Lombok, women use the clay found in local riverbeds to create rich, red-brown pieces of pottery. They shape the clay with their hands, stones, and wooden paddles, often adding delicate designs carved with a sharp bamboo stick.

Mothers pass their basket-weaving skills and knowledge to their daughters. Many kinds of plant fibers are used, including reed, grass, bamboo, rattan, and palms. From these plants, women make hats, boxes, baskets, bags, and mats.

The Ceremonies of Life

Many of life's events are causes of celebration in Indonesia. Although traditions vary depending on location and religion, most are met with enthusiasm and emotion.

Children are cherished in Indonesia. Since the country has a relatively high infant mortality rate, babies who do survive are treasured. When a woman is three months pregnant in Bali, or seven months pregnant in Java and Sudan, she is given a ritual bath called a *tujah bulan*. Surrounded by women, she is loved, supported, prayed for, bathed in scented water, and given flowers. Traditionally, she serves a very spicy fruit salad to her guests. The comments they make about it are supposed to be indications of whether the baby will be a boy or a girl and what his or her personality will be like.

After a baby is born, some groups of Indonesian women will rest at home for 30 to 40 days. When they are ready, an announcement is made and visitors come with gifts and good wishes. A Batak mother makes a special rice cake on the seventh day after birth and takes it to the village to share the cake and to show her baby the sun for the first time. Amulets are often placed around a child's arms or neck to ward off evil spirits and danger.

When a Muslim boy is between five and eleven, he is circumcized in a ceremony called the *sunatan*. Many of these operations are performed in the hospital, but some groups still do it in their villages. In East Java, the boys ride a horse throughout the village streets afterward and are given money.

Helping the Children

In Indonesia, the face of Christine Hakim is a familiar one. She has not only made more than thirty films in Southeast Asia but also has dedicated a great deal of her time and energy to helping Indonesia's children. Through the Christine Hakim foundation, milk is supplied to hundreds of needy children in West Java and Aceh. In addition, the organization provides funds to update schools and to pay teachers.

In 2004, Hakim sometimes referred to as the Elizabeth Taylor of Indonesia, took on the role of ambassador for the United Nations Children's Fund in Indonesia. "Although it will be a tough job, it is a great honor for me as I can play an active role in promoting the welfare of Indonesian children," said Hakim.

Childhood ends when a young adult decides to marry. Engagements may last years, as couples finish their schooling or work to raise money for their marriage. For an Indonesian not to get married is considered a tragedy.

Weddings are lavish ceremonies with huge crowds. Often the bride and groom are put on thrones, and guests file by to offer good wishes and gifts. Chinese women wear long, white gowns, while Javanese women wear fine white blouses with

This bride and groom are placed on a throne and wear ornate gold jewelry.

Death with the Torajan

The death customs of the Torajan in Sulawesi are unusual. When a person dies, the preparations for the celebration may take months. During that time, the deceased remains in the home with family and is visited by honored members of the village. Funerals last from one to seven days, depending on the person's status within the community. The events are considered to be parties, complete with dancing, sports, and music. The deceased is put inside a high tower to watch over the celebration.

A number of buffalo are killed during the funeral. The Torajan believe that the dead are taken to the afterlife on the souls of buffalo, so the more that are killed, the easier the ride will be. It also means fresh meat for the region.

When it comes time for burial, the deceased is taken to a cliff, where it will be put inside a cave or even a large, hollow tree. A life-sized effigy, or *tau tau*, of that person is carefully placed on a balcony that has been carved into the side of a cliff. Its clothing will be replaced every twenty-five years.

---

batik. The Batak put numerous scarves across their shoulders, and the Minangkabau wear ornate gold headdresses.

The reception following the wedding is often immense. Thousands of people—even strangers—come from all over to attend. It is not unusual for a family to have to sell land or livestock in order to pay for the cost of the reception.

Funerals in Indonesia are often announced by yellow paper flags tied to all the trees and poles in a community. For Muslims, the time period from death to grave is usually less than 24 hours. When word goes out that a Muslim has died, people drop everything and rush to attend to the family. Not to do so would dishonor the family. With a group present, the body is stripped, washed, put on a woven mat, and wrapped in three layers of cloth. After prayers are said, the body is carried to the cemetery on the shoulders of friends or in a car. The Muslim is placed in a grave with his head pointing toward Mecca, and people file by to drop in flowers and dirt.

A Day in the Life

WHEN BABIES ARE BORN IN INDONESIA, THEY ARE HELD and carried almost every hour of the day. As they grow, they are carried in a *selendang*, or a sling made of cloth tied around the shoulder of mothers or older siblings. For the first year or two of life, the baby is kept in the sling during the day to nurse when hungry, sleep when tired, and just be near someone who loves him. This method of parenting symbolizes how Indonesians approach life in general. Families are very important; they are the source of comfort, help, and support. They are there for *hangat*, or warmth of body and spirit.

Opposite: **Families are an important element of daily life in Indonesia.**

Time to Eat!

Thanks to the influence of all the different cultures, Indonesian food is incredibly varied. The typical dishes made in homes and restaurants reflect the influences of India, China, Arab nations, Holland, Japan, and Thailand. Strangely enough, the spices that the islands are so well known for, from cinnamon to nutmeg, are rarely used in Indonesian cuisine. Instead, they usually spice their meals with hot chili peppers.

The durian is a favorite fruit for many Indonesians.

The people of Indonesia eat a lot of fruit, from the familiar watermelon and forty different kinds of bananas to the less familiar guava, mango, and rambutan. Another favorite is the durian, which looks like a football with spikes on the outside and scrambled eggs on the inside. The smell is like dirty socks—and yet many people enjoy the unusual flavor. The meat and juice of the coconut are treats, and the oil is often used in cooking. Surrounded by rivers and oceans, Indonesians eat a great deal of fish and other seafood such as eel, lobster, and shrimp. The lush rain forests provide them with the leaves of the bamboo and cassava and the edible flowers of the hibiscus and banana tree.

The one food that is found in almost every single meal on every single day is rice. It truly is the staple food of the Indonesian culture. It is put on the side of fish or meat, covered by vegetables or eggs, or baked into desserts.

On the streets of many cities throughout Indonesia, the special call of the *kaki lima* can be heard. These food vendors have moving carts that they push up and down the sidewalk. Each one has its own special call, from the ring of a bell to brass wind chimes. As soon as they see someone look their way, they pull their walking restaurant over and begin cooking. Stationary sidewalk restaurants called *warungs* are snack bars with a counter and a bench for customers.

Time for Some Peanut Sauce!

Spicy peanut sauce is used in many different recipes in Indonesia, as well as in Malaysia and Thailand. It is considered a condiment much like ketchup is in the United States. Here is how to make it:

Ingredients:

$\frac{1}{4}$ c crunchy peanut butter

$\frac{1}{4}$ c soy sauce

$\frac{1}{4}$ c lime juice

$\frac{1}{4}$ c rice vinegar

3 T freshly chopped coriander

1 T brown sugar

$\frac{1}{4}$ t chili flakes

Directions: Over low heat, warm the peanut butter and stir in the soy sauce, lime juice, and rice vinegar until it is all smooth. Add the coriander, brown sugar, and chili flakes. Stir until everything is completely mixed and serve it warm. It is good over rice, mixed vegetables, or for meat.

Although forks, spoons, and knives are used, Indonesians prefer to eat with their bare hands. Food is always eaten and passed with the right hand, whether at the kitchen table or in the fanciest restaurant. The left hand is considered unclean and not to be used.

The Evolution of Clothing

At one time, the clothes an Indonesian wore told much about his or her ethnic background, social status, and other important details. Today, those living in the larger cities wear the typical clothing of Westerners, from dresses and suits to jeans and

Traditional Indonesian dress

T-shirts. In the more rural areas, traditional clothing can still be seen. In the western islands, the colorful and bright batik is worn, while in the east, intricate ikat designs are common.

Muslims wear clothes that reflect their faith. Women commonly cover their heads with a veil. A long tunic is worn over loose trousers. Other times, they may wear tight, long-sleeved shirts and a sarong, or long piece of fabric tied around the waist as a long skirt.

Muslim men also wear sarongs but knot them differently over pants. They frequently add a dark waistcoat, or vest, over the top. Many also wear a *pici*, or black velvet cap.

Some of the more remote islands have much different styles of dress. For instance, the people of Irian Jaya do not wear many clothes at all. Women tend to wear only grass skirts, while men wear only penis sheaths.

Home, Sweet Home

In Indonesia's biggest cities, the skyscrapers and other buildings look much like those in Western cities. In the rural areas, however, most of the houses are built on stilts to protect them from floodwaters and heavy rains. The open spaces under the homes provide shelter for domestic animals like chickens and pigs, as well as the wild rodents or reptiles that might be passing through.

Most homes are built out of wood and bamboo, with palm thatches for the roof. Some ethnic groups decorate the exterior with bamboo lattices, geometric designs, or carved sculptures. Those who still practice animism often

In Kalimantan, homes are built on stilts to protect them from rising water.

believe that their homes are living creatures with their own spirits and consider the roof as the sacred place where ancestors are to be honored.

Receiving an education in Indonesia is expensive

Off to School—or Not

Before the huge financial crisis of 1997, school enrollment in Indonesia was averaging 90 percent for children under twelve, but afterward, that number dropped dramatically. School is not free in this country, and for many families, the cost of books, tuition, and uniforms is more than they can afford. Those children who are not in school spend their days working in the fields or helping their families in shops and at home.

Public schools are broken into three levels: primary school from ages six to twelve, junior high from twelve to fifteen, and senior high from fifteen to eighteen. Less than half of the children in primary school will go on to junior high. Less than half of those will stay long enough to graduate. The problem is further complicated by an ongoing teacher shortage, especially on the less populated islands.

Some mosques and churches sponsor private schools, but the fees are high and only the wealthy can afford them. Colleges, such as the Universitas Indonesia in Jakarta and the Universitas Gajah Mada in Yogyakarta, are also quite expensive.

Festivals of All Kinds

Since Indonesia is rich with religious diversity, it also celebrates a variety of sacred holidays. The majority of people are Islamic, and one of the biggest holidays is Ramadan. For one month, men, women and even older children fast, or stop eating, drinking, and smoking, from sunrise to sunset to test religious faith and self-discipline. When Ramadan ends, *Idul Fitri*, or Lebaran, begins and lasts from one week to a month. Muslims celebrate with feasting, gift-giving, and fireworks. This is also the time that they ask for forgiveness from their elders for any mistakes or offense given in the past. They greet each other with "*Selamat Idul Fitri, Ma'afkan Lahir Batin*," which means "Happy Idul Fitri and forgive us for all our wrongdoings." Because Islamic holidays are based on a lunar calendar, instead of the traditional solar one, their dates shift about eleven days each year.

Hindu festivals are celebrated on Bali, and the biggest of all is *Nyepi*, the Hindu New Year. On the eve of Nyepi, the Hindus make as much noise as possible with gongs and cymbals to drive away demons. The next day, they stay home and are silent to convince any remaining demons the city is deserted. Also called the Day of Complete Silence, it is spent praying and meditating.

Waisak is the most important festival for the Buddhists. It celebrates the birth, enlightenment, and death of Buddha. Thousands of people gather at Borobudur and watch as monks offer up flowers, fruit, and prayers.

Indonesian Buddhist monks celebrate the Buddha's birthday at Borobudur

Independence Day parade

Chinese Indonesians celebrate their new year, Imlek. They hand out moon cakes, fly kites, and have a dragon parade. They also go to temple to pray to their ancestors.

Christians celebrate Christmas in a traditional way. Easter, however, is quite different. On the island of Flores, the celebration begins at midnight with a candlelight parade, drums, grass pom-poms, and torches. A black coffin to symbolize the death of Jesus and a statue of the Virgin Mary are carried throughout the parade.

The only national holiday in Indonesia is Independence Day in August. Flag-raising ceremonies occur in many parts of the country, and flags are displayed in people's houses, cars, stores, and businesses. There are games, sporting events, parades, and other celebrations, including music and dancing.

It's Holiday Time in Indonesia

January 1	New Year's Day
January or February	Imlek (Chinese New Year)
January	Idul Adha (return of pilgrims from Mecca)
January or February	Muharram (Islamic New Year)
March or April	Good Friday
March or April	Easter
March or April	Nyepi (Balinese New Year)
April or May	Maulud Nabi Muhammed (birthday of the prophet)
May	Waisak Day (Buddha's birth, enlightenment, and death)
May	Ascension of Christ
August 17	Hari Proklamasi Kemerdekaan/Independence Day
August or September	Isra Miraj Nabi Muhammed (ascension of the prophet)
October or November	Idul Fitri or Lebaran (end of Ramadan)
December 25	Hari Natal/Christmas Day

Susi Susanti at the 1992 Olympic Games

Play Ball!

One of the Indonesian government's mottoes is "Sports for All!" and each September they celebrate National Sports Day. Games of all kinds are popular throughout the archipelago, and the country is known internationally for its badminton players. Two favorites are Susi Susanti and Alan Budi Kusuma, a married couple who both won Olympic gold medals in 1992. In 2004, they both were part of the torch relay for the Olympics held in Athens. Other famous players include Rudy Hartono, eight-time winner of the All England Badminton Championship, and Ellyas Pical, a prizewinning boxer.

Stone jumping proves
courage and strength.

From Champion to Coach

In 1995, a tall, slim man named Joko Suprianto returned to Indonesia with the World Cup and World Grand Prix titles in badminton. He was greeted with great pride, parades, and parties. In Indonesia, badminton is a hugely popular sport that does not faintly resemble the gentle backyard games some may imagine. Here the game depends on speed, skill, and fast reactions. Indonesia has led the game in many international sporting competitions. That was true at the 2004 Olympics, where Suprianto worked not as a player, but as the coach for the Indonesian team. "The team has a commitment to win and that's what we're planning to do," says Suprianto.

On Nias Island, west of Sumatra, the sport of stone jumping is quite popular with young men. Based on the ancient art of training warriors for battle, the goal is to run and jump over a 5-foot-high, 1.5-foot wide (1.5 m by 0.5 m) stone wall and land safely on the other side. Some even perform the feat with a sword in hand.

Other popular sports include *sepak takraw*, a game similar to volleyball (except the ball is woven out of rattan) and *pencak silat*, a martial arts sport that is a lot like karate. The 6.2-mile (10-km) Paradise Run in Bali attracts runners from all over the world. Many come to see the Madurese annual bull runs.

A Game by Many Names

One game that is played through Indonesia is *congklat*. Some version of it is played all over the world, although by different names. In Africa, it is *wari*. In Arabic countries, it is mancala, and in England, it is Count and Capture. Some islands play it for fun, while others follow the tradition of only playing it while in mourning.

The playing board is made out of wood and has five to nine holes on each side. The boards vary from plain to intricately carved and painted pieces in the shape of boats or dragons. The playing pieces can be seeds, shells, or stones. Players need ninety-eight of them. The object of the game is to get as many pieces as you can into your storehouse, the hole at the end of the board on the left. The game continues until one player loses all his pieces or until both people want to stop.

Timeline

Indonesian History		World History
Java Man migrates to Indonesia.	1,000,000–500,000 B.C.	
Modern humans migrate to Indonesia.	40,000–30,000 B.C.	
Indonesians begin to practice farming.	10,000 B.C.	
Migrants from Malay Peninsula and China introduce tools, utensils, and bronze.	3,000 B.C.	
	2500 B.C.	Egyptians build the Pyramids and the Sphinx in Giza.
Indian traders arrive in Indonesia and introduce Buddhism and Hinduism.	500 B.C.	
	563 B.C.	The Buddha is born in India.
	A.D. 313	The Roman emperor Constantine recognizes Christianity.
Arab traders arrive in Indonesia and introduce Islam.	About A.D. 700	610	The Prophet Muhammad begins preaching a new religion called Islam.
	1054	The Eastern (Orthodox) and Western (Roman) Churches break apart.
	1066	William the Conqueror defeats the English in the Battle of Hastings.
	1095	Pope Urban II proclaims the First Crusade.
	1215	King John seals the Magna Carta.
Golden Age of Majapahit Empire.	1292–1527	
	1300s	The Renaissance begins in Italy.
	1347	The Black Death sweeps through Europe.
	1453	Ottoman Turks capture Constantinople, conquering the Byzantine Empire.
	1492	Columbus arrives in North America.
	1500s	The Reformation leads to the birth of Protestantism.
The Portuguese capture Malacca.	1511	
The first Dutch ships arrive in Indonesia.	1596	
The Dutch build Batavia (present-day Jakarta).	1618	
	1776	The Declaration of Independence is signed.
	1789	The French Revolution begins.

128 *Indonesia*

Indonesian History

There is a period of English rule under Sir Thomas S. Raffles.	1811–1815
The Java War is fought against the Dutch.	1825–1830
Sukarno founds the first major political party with the goal of independence.	1927
Japan rules Indonesia.	1942–1945
Sukarno declares Indonesia's independence.	1945
The Dutch acknowledge Indonesia's independence.	1949
Sukarno declares himself Supreme Ruler for Life.	1963
A coup is attempted; anti-communist/anti-Chinese riots occur.	1965
Suharto takes over the presidency.	1967
Indonesia annexes East Timor.	1976
An economic crisis hits Indonesia.	1997
Suharto resigns; B. J. Habibie becomes the third president.	1998
Indonesia holds its first democratic election in forty years, Abdurrahman Wahid becomes fourth president; East Timor votes for independence.	1999
Wahid is impeached; Megawati Sukarnoputri becomes the fifth president.	2001
Islamic terrorists explode bombs on Bali.	2002
The second free election since 1955 occurs; and Susilo Bambang Yudhoyona is voted president.	2004

World History

1865	The American Civil War ends.
1914	World War I breaks out.
1917	The Bolshevik Revolution brings communism to Russia.
1929	Worldwide economic depression begins.
1939	World War II begins, following the German invasion of Poland.
1945	World War II ends.
1957	The Vietnam War starts.
1969	Humans land on the moon.
1975	The Vietnam War ends.
1979	Soviet Union invades Afghanistan.
1983	Drought and famine in Africa.
1989	The Berlin Wall is torn down, as communism crumbles in Eastern Europe.
1991	Soviet Union breaks into separate states.
1992	Bill Clinton is elected U.S. president.
2000	George W. Bush is elected U.S. president.
2001	Terrorists attack World Trade Towers, New York and the Pentagon, Washington, D.C.
2003	A coalition of forty-nine nations, headed by the United States and Great Britain, invade Iraq.

Fast Facts

Official name: Republic of Indonesia

Capital: Jakarta

Official language: Bahasa Indonesia

Jakarta

Indonesia's flag

Mahakam River

Official religion:	Islam
Year of founding:	1945
National anthem:	*Indonesia Raya* ("Great Indonesia")
Government:	Republic
Chief of state:	President
Head of government:	President
Area:	741,097 square miles (1,919,440 sq km)
Coordinate of geographical center:	5 00' S, 120 00' E
Dimensions:	1,200 miles (1,930 km) north to south 3,200 miles (5,150 km) east to west
Bordering countries:	East Timor, Malaysia, Papua New Guinea
Bordering water:	South China Sea (north); North Pacific Ocean (north/east); Indian Ocean (south/west)
Highest elevation:	Puncak Jaya, 16,503 feet (5,030 m)
Lowest elevation:	Indian Ocean, 0 feet (0 m)
Average temperatures:	80°F (27°C) and 70°F (21°C)
Average annual rainfall:	177 inches (450 cm) in the mountains 51 inches (130 cm) in the lowlands

Hindu temples

Currency

National population (2004 est.): 238,452,952

Population of largest cities:

Jakarta in Java	12,296,000
Bandung in Java	3,409,000
Surabaya in Java	2,461,000
Medan in Sumatra	2,204,300
Menarang in Java	1,267,100

Famous landmarks:
- ▶ *Borobudur*, Java
- ▶ *Monas*, Jakarta
- ▶ *Prambanan*, Java

Industry: Indonesia's most important product is natural gas, followed by coal and oil. The country's manufacturing plants make cement, fertilizers, paper and plywood, and textiles. Other important products include coffee, rice, and rubber. Tourism is climbing, after taking a serious dip following the 2002 bombings in Bali.

Currency: As of January 7, 2005, 9,677 rupiah were equal to U.S.$1.

Weights and measures: Indonesia uses the metric system.

Literacy: Total population: 87.9%
Male: 92.5%
Female: 83.4%

Man selling Wayang puppets

Sukarno

Common Indonesian words and phrases:

Namanya siapa?	What is your name?
Senagn ketemu.	Nice to meet you.
Dari mana?	Where are you from?
Agama anda apa?	What is your religion?
Berapa harganya?	How much does this cost?
Jam berapa sekarang?	What time is it?
Terima kasih.	Thank you.
Ma'af.	I'm sorry.
Sampai jumpa lagi.	Till we meet again.

Famous Indonesians:

Anwar Chairil (1922–1949)
Famous writer/author

Raden Adjeng Kartin (1879–1904)
First spokesperson for women's rights

Suharto (1921–)
Second president of Indonesia

Sukarno (1901–1970)
First president of Indonesia

Pangeran Diponigoro (1785–1855)
Javanese leader

Didik Nini Thowok (1954–)
Internationally known dancer and teacher

To Find Out More

Books

- Corwin, Jeff. *Into Wild Indonesia.* San Diego: Blackbirch Press, 2004.

- Cumming, David and Julio Etchart. *Indonesia.* United Kingdom: Cherrytree Books, 2004.

- Daley, Patrick. *Indonesia.* Chicago: Raintree Books, 2002.

- Furgang, Kathy. *Krakatoa: History's Loudest Volcano.* New York: PowerKids Press, 2001.

- Guile, Melanie. *Culture in Indonesia.* Chicago: Raintree Books, 2003.

- Horton, Edward. *Indonesia.* Chicago: Raintree Books, 2004.

- Phillips, Douglas. *Indonesia.* Broomall, PA: Chelsea House Publishers, 2004.

- Riehecky, Janet. *Indonesia.* Mankato, Minnesota: Bridgestone Books, 2002.

- Simpson, Judith. *Indonesia.* Broomall, PA: Mason Crest Publishers, 2002.

Web Sites

▶ **The World Factbook: Indonesia**
www.cia.gov/cia/publications/
factbook/geos/id.html
*Statistical information about
Indonesia's geography, people,
government, and economy.*

▶ **Introduction to Indonesia**
www.interknowledge.com/
indonesia/
*General information on Indonesia's
history, culture, geography,
and climate.*

Organizations

▶ **Embassy of the Republic of
Indonesia**
2020 Massachusetts Avenue, NW
Washington, DC 20036

▶ **United States Indonesia Society**
1625 Massachusetts Avenue, NW
Suite 550
Washington, DC 20236-2260

Index

Page numbers in *italics* indicate illustrations.

religion and, 48, 95
structure of, 61–63
Sukarno and, 54, 55–56
Government Party, 63
Greater Sunda Islands, 21–22
"guided democracy", 54
Gusmao, Jose Alexandre
"Xanana", 66

H

Habibie, B. J., 57, 65
hajj (pilgrimage), 99
Hakim, Christine, 113
Hartono, Rudy, 125
Hindu-Buddhist kingdoms, *45*, 46–47
Hinduism, 10, 46, 86, 99, 100, 122–123
holidays. *see* festivals and holidays
Holland. *see* Dutch rule
Homo erectus, 43
Homo floresiensis, 44
hot springs, 19
House of People's Representatives, 61
housing, 68, 84, 88, 120–121
human rights, 56, 59

I

ikat (fabric knotting), 110, 119
Imlek (holiday), 124
Independence Day, 124
independence movements, 43
against Dutch, 51
from Indonesia, 57, 64–67
Java War, 52
literature and, 103, 104
Sukarno and, 54
Indianized kingdoms, 45–46
Indian Ocean, 15
Indonesia, name of, 15
Indonesian Nationalist Party, 65
Indonesian Observer (newspaper), 79
insects, 38

international aid, 18, 66, 77, 113
Internet, the, 79
Irianese people, 89
Irian Jaya (province), 25, 28, 66–67,
89, 92, 120
Islam, 9, 95–99
clothing and, 119–120
funerals and, 115
government and, 57, 63
holidays, 122
origins of, 46, 47–48
islands, 10, 15, 21–23, 25
see also specific islands

J

jaipongan music, 106
Jakarta, *10*, 68–69, *69*
Jakarta Post (newspaper), 79
Japanese rule, 43, 53–54
Java (island), 10, 21, 22, 76, 82–84
Java Man, *43*, 43–44
Javanese people, 82–83, 114–115
Java War, 52
Jayakarta (kingdom), 50
jobs. *see* employment
Joko Suprianto, 127
judicial branch, 62–63

K

kaki lima (food vendors), 118
Kalimantan (province), 15–17, 21, 23,
88–89
Kalla, Jusef, 64
kampungs (neighborhoods), 68
Kartini, Raden Ajeng, 52
Kasada, ceremony of, 101
Keli Mutu (volcano), 20–21
keris (dagger), 109, *109*
Komodo dragons, 40, *40*
Krakatoa (volcano), 27
Kusuma, Alan Budi, 125

Meet the Author

TAMRA ORR is a full-time writer and author living in Portland, Oregon. She has written almost fifty nonfiction books for children and families, including Enchantment of the World *Turkey* and *Slovenia* for Children's Press.

Writing about a country that is made up of almost endless islands and so much diversity in its people was fascinating for Orr. Imagining a place this beautiful and yet so different from one place to another was intriguing. It was not long before she was thinking about packing her own bags and trying to figure out how to move to one of those many uninhabited islands and see them all firsthand.

Photo Credits

akg-Images, London: 49 top

AP/Wide World Photos: 96 (Charles Dharapak), 103 (Suzanne Plunkett), 28 (Pikiran Rakyat)

Art Resource, NY/Giraudon/Palazzo Farnese, Caprarola, Italy: 47 top

Bridgeman Art Library International Ltd., London/New York: 51 (London Zoological Society, UK), 100, 132 top

Corbis Images: 37 top (Theo Allofs), 76 top (Yann Arthus-Bertrand), 64 (Beawiharta/Reuters), 43, 55 bottom, 65, 133 bottom (Bettmann), 30 (Tom Brakefield), 41 (Brandon D. Cole), 70 (Dean Conger), 76 bottom (Sergio Dorantes), 50 top (Edifice), 24 top (Reinhard Eisele), 16 (Jack Fields), 109 (Werner Forman), 83, 116 (Owen Franken), 2 (Peter Guttman), 61 (Tarmizy Harva/Reuters), cover, 6, 47 bottom, 85, 102, 106 (Lindsay Hebberd), 20, 72, 132 bottom (Jeremy Horner), 24 bottom (Dave G. Houser), 42 (Hulton-Deutsch Collection), 31, 40, 74, 110 (Wolfgang Kaehler), 78 (Dan Lamont), 9, 11, 19, 84, 89, 98, 126 (Charles & Josette Lenars), 38 (Buddy Mays), 18 (Yuriko Nakao/Reuters), 123 (Dwi Obli/Reuters), 17, 88, 131 bottom (Charles O'Rear), 94 (Christine Osborne), 63 (Crack Palinggi/Reuters), 67 top (Reuters), 87 (Anders Ryman), 25 (Albrecht G. Schaefer), 36 (Keren Su), 57, 58 (Supri/Reuters), 12 (The Cover Story), 56 (Peter Turnley), 10, 79 bottom, 130 left (Nik Wheeler), 59 (Darren Whiteside/Reuters), 34 (Michael S. Yamashita)

Corbis Sygma/Jufri Kemal: 66

Envision Stock Photography Inc./ Sharon Smith: 117

Getty Images/Shaun Botterill: 125

Hulton | Archive/Getty Images: 27, 53 top, 55 top

Minden Pictures: 37 bottom (Tui De Roy), 33 (Frans Lanting)

NASA/Jeff Schmaltz/MODIS Rapid Response Team/GSFC: 14

Network Aspen: 92 (Jeffrey Aaronsen), 73 bottom (Geoffrey Clifford), 8 (Jones & Shimlock)

Panos Pictures: 111 (Jeremy Hartley), 22 (Fred Hoogervorst), 121 (Marcus Rose), 68 top, 93, 97 (Chris Stowers)

Peter Arnold Inc./John Paul Kay: 60

The Art Archive/Picture Desk: 48 (British Library), 53 bottom (Dagli Orti/Domenica del Corniere), 7 bottom, 108 (Dagli Orti/Rijksmuseum voor Volkenkunde Leiden)

The Image Works: 32, 35 (Michael J. Doolittle), 105 (Hideo Haga), 91 (Edy Purnomo), 50 bottom (Topham)

TRIP Photo Library: 39 (M. Both), 23 (C.C.), 120 (Colin Conway), 80, 133 top (J. Greenberg), 68 bottom (Tim Lester), 7 top, 77 (P. Mercea), 79 top, 112 (Robin Nichols), 99 (H. Rogers), 107, 124 (J. Sweeney), 119 (Adina Tovy), 114 (J. Wakelin)

Maps by XNR Productions Inc.